★ ★ ★ ★ ★

VIETNAM AND CHRISTIANITY

★ ★ ★ ★ ★

A Vietnam Veteran's Transformation from Army Soldier to Warrior of God

DON BOUDREAUX

★★★★★

VIETNAM AND CHRISTIANITY

★★★★★

A Vietnam Veteran's Transformation from Army Soldier to Warrior of God

Published by Redemption Press, PO Box 427, Enumclaw, WA 98022.

Toll-Free (844) 2REDEEM (273-3336)

Redemption Press is honored to present this title in partnership with the author. The views expressed or implied in this work are those of the author. Redemption Press provides our imprint seal representing design excellence, creative content, and high quality production.

The author has tried to recreate events, locales, and conversations from memories of them. In order to maintain their anonymity, in some instances the names of individuals are changed and some identifying characteristics and details may have changed, such as physical properties, occupations, and places of residence.

ISBN 13: 978-1-64645-218-7 (Paperback)
978-1-64645-219-4 (ePub)
978-1-64645-220-0 (Mobi)

Library of Congress Catalog Card Number: 2020922217

DEDICATION

I dedicate this book, first and foremost, to my Lord and Savior, Jesus Christ, who has been so faithful in my life. I also honor my wonderful family, who are all my most cherished blessings from God: my loving wife and called prophetess, Sheila, who diligently prayed and encouraged me throughout the writing and publishing of this book, as well as my precious children. Further, I am deeply grateful to Kim Silva, my cooperative rewrite editor, who did an outstanding job in aiding me to transform my story from my disjointed notes to this book, and I praise Jesus and sincerely thank all members of the Redemption Press team for their patience and diligence as they labored to publish my work. I want to specifically thank my son, Joshua, for his tireless work to assist me in writing this book.

Vietnam and Christianity is also dedicated to American veterans of all generations for their selfless contributions on the battlefront and the home front—protectors of the greatest nation on earth—and to healthcare professionals throughout the world who devote their lives to helping those in need. Lastly, I dedicate this book to all those who have contributed to my spiritual growth, especially Pastor Jimmy Lopez, who ordained and licensed me as a minister.

★ ★

INTRODUCTION

I ENTERED THE MILITARY AT age seventeen. I wanted to experience war like my father did in World War II. Though I didn't know God at the time, He knew my wartime experiences would come to represent more than physical war: in retrospect, He wanted me to learn war in the natural realm so I could later correlate my experiences to war in the spiritual realm. However, the Lord did not only send me to the Vietnam War to simply help me to understand the correlations between physical and Spiritual warfare, He sent me there to prepare me to actually fight the Spiritual war against Satan that was soon to begin for me.

The earliest records of war date around 2700 BC, and the first battle recorded in the Bible is found in Genesis 14. Later in the Old Testament, King David fought against the Philistines, and Moses and the children of Israel fought against the Amorites, the Perizzites, the Hivites, the Jebusites, the Hittites, the Girgashites, and the Canaanites. Father God wanted His people to fight the wicked and make the earth righteous.

We still war in the natural realm today, and we will continue to do so until the Lord of hosts (armies), Jehovah Sabaoth, comes back (Matthew 24:6). He is the God of war. Exodus 15:3 says, "The LORD is a man of war: the LORD is his name." Though in many cases the motives of human rulers for initiating war have been quite evil over the centuries, God's motives for starting wars and conquests are perfectly pure and just. For instance, God says to the Israelites, "Not for thy righteousness, or for the uprightness of thine heart, dost thou go to possess their land: but for the wickedness of these nations the Lord thy God doth drive them out from before thee, and that he may perform the word which the Lord sware unto thy fathers, Abraham, Isaac, and Jacob" (Deuteronomy 9:5). The Lord is saying here that His purpose in destroying the nations for Israel was not because of the righteousness of the Israelites but because He desired to punish the wickedness of the nations that He was destroying. Since we know that God justly punishes the wicked (Ezekiel 18:25–26; Romans 13:1–4), it is clear to see that God's motives for war are completely pure, not driven by desire for selfish gain. But though I embrace my God as a warrior, I am grateful He is also a God of peace: "And the God of peace shall bruise Satan under your feet shortly. The grace of our Lord Jesus Christ be with you. Amen" (Romans 16:20).

While not all of us will experience natural and physical warfare, we are all subject to spiritual warfare and need to be on the lookout: "Be sober, be vigilant; because your adversary the devil, as a roaring lion, walketh about, seeking whom he may devour" (1 Peter 5:8). My experience in Vietnam and my life as a follower of Jesus have opened my eyes to the spiritual wars that all believers fight.

It's been decades since I fought in Vietnam, and now I love to read what God's Word says about war and soldiers. I'm amazed at how my service in Vietnam correlates to my life as a born-again Christian. I have written this book to recount some of my experiences in military combat and to explain how strategies and experiences of military soldiers correlate to the reality of spiritual warfare for Christians. My experiences were not mere coincidences. Father God wanted those events to happen in my life, and He arranged everything. Even when I was not yet saved, He arranged my going to Vietnam through the US Army. Years later I became a

Christian, a true disciple of the Lord Jesus Christ. The word *disciple* means "learner." I am in an ongoing learning process. He wants us all to become His disciples and come to the knowledge of the truth.

I am proud to have represented the United States of America in Vietnam. Just as the word *united* is in the title of our country, we need to be united in the Lord Jesus. Proverbs 18:14 (AMPC) says, "The strong spirit of a man sustains him in bodily pain or trouble, but a weak *and* broken spirit who can raise up or bear?" The vast majority of people in this country, whom I love, need to be born again through Jesus to have a strong spirit. Once we are born again, our spirits need to be fed all the time, day and night, as the Lord told Joshua in Joshua 1:8, "This book of the law shall not depart out of thy mouth; but thou shalt meditate therein day and night, that thou mayest observe to do according to all that is written therein: for then thou shalt make thy way prosperous, and then thou shalt have good success."

It is my hope and prayer that everyone becomes born again in Jesus. I especially have a tender spot for those who have seen the inside of a military uniform—all current members of the military as well as veterans of all the branches of service, along with their spouses—to become born again and call upon His name to be saved. "Look unto me, and be ye saved, all the ends of the earth: for I am God, and there is none else" (Isaiah 45:22).

I pray in Jesus's name that the Lord moves on all people to read this book because it is God inspired. The Bible, of course, is the ultimate inspiration of God. Every word in the Bible is fully inspired by the Holy Spirit of God, and there has never or never will be a book written like it. Further, the Word of God is the only book from which we can most reliably understand God's ways, character, and attributes.

When I say God inspired me to write this book, I mean the Lord told me thirty years ago to write a book. I was an uneducated man at the time and didn't trust I was hearing Him right, so I told Him I needed confirmation. About thirty years later, a prophetess (female prophet) I didn't even know told me to write a book. That was my confirmation. The Lord gave me ideas for the writing of this book to encourage Christians to fight the good fight of faith and to offer unbelievers an opportunity to turn to Jesus through the reading of my experiences in Vietnam. The Lord is good, and His mercy endures forever (Psalm 100:5). If it were not for Him, I would not have written this book.

I hope this book comes into the hands of warriors, soldiers, Marines, sailors, airmen, and anybody else who can relate to my story. I didn't write this book primarily for profit, but for the sake of heaven and for the love of Jesus my Lord.

There is no other religion in the world that offers eternal life to enjoy Jesus Christ forever. Jesus was crucified and raised and is alive in heaven today. Think on this one thing: Jesus is the Savior of the whole world. There is no other Savior.

Because of the Lord Jesus, I am more military minded now than I ever was when I was in the army and even in Vietnam. Today, I am militant for my Lord, and I am His soldier and warrior. He makes the difference by His blood, the blood of the Lamb of God slain from the foundation of the world. "And all that dwell upon the earth shall worship him, whose names are not written in the book of life of the Lamb slain from the foundation of the world" (Revelation 13:8).

★ ★ CHAPTER 1

GROWING UP AND GOING TO WAR

Whoso loveth instruction loveth knowledge: but he that hateth reproof is brutish.

Proverbs 12:1

AFTER DROPPING OUT OF SCHOOL twice, I never thought I'd become an ordained minister and a called prophet. A former pastor once called me a late bloomer. I bloomed, matured, and flourished once I met my Savior.

I was born in 1949 in the small town of Rayne, Louisiana, to Hampton Boudreaux Jr. and Bertha S. Boudreaux (née Simon). My parents and three siblings and I only went to church on Christmas Eve. My parents talked to us about God occasionally, but no one in my family was a Christian, and I didn't know what it meant to be born again.

My parents divorced when I was twelve. My father pursued other women while still married to my mother, and he drank heavily. I remember going to the honkey-tonks with him, even when I was a young child. Bar fights were commonplace. Once he asked a barmaid to watch me while he indulged in a bar fight; I cried in the corner as he fought.

After my parents' divorce, I didn't spend as much time with him, but when I was an adult and we did spend time together, it was usually in a bar. Later in life, I learned that though I didn't have a reliable earthly father, I have a heavenly Father who loves and cares for me: "And will be a Father unto you, and ye shall be my sons and daughters, saith the Lord Almighty" (2 Corinthians 6:18).

I spent a lot of my youth doing my own thing and getting drunk whenever I could. I was headstrong, and like my father I was drawn to partying. One of my uncles tried to keep me on the straight and narrow and provide a firm hand, but I was too bullheaded to accept his guidance and boundaries, and I continued to live how I wanted to live, not listening to or obeying anyone.

School never came easy for me, so I decided to drop out . . . twice. I first left school at age fifteen but thought better of it and gave it another try. I dropped out again for good at age seventeen. Immature and uneducated, I had no direction for my life. My mother wasn't happy about my decision, and she knew that finding employment without an education would be difficult, so she took immediate action to get me enlisted in the army. She called my father, who was living in Port Arthur, Texas, at the time. He took me to Lafayette, Louisiana, where I signed up for the US Army and became a military man.

I had basic training for eight weeks at Fort Polk, Louisiana. Military personnel receive extensive training. Basic training is as grueling as its reputation. The physical training and proficiency tests were challenging, requiring us to meet certain thresholds for running and exercising in our combat boots and fatigues. If we failed, we'd have to recycle, or restart, basic training. We also had close-order drills in basic training, learning how to follow orders and memorize proper army protocols. Our superiors would holler orders such as "left face," "right face," "left-shoulder arms," "right-shoulder arms," and I'd struggle because I wasn't used to listening carefully to instructions. I also struggled with weapons training. I was a bad shot and found it hard to get used to the report and recoil of the M-14 rifle. It was startling to me, to say the least. I learned a lot about discipline with tasks such as ensuring my boots were shined and my bed was made correctly. But by far the hardest part of basic training was enduring as my superiors yelled in my face when I disobeyed orders or acted in a way they did not appreciate. They'd demand pushups or harsher disciplinary action while hollering inches away from me. Unfortunately, too many squad leaders misused their authority by giving unnecessary and unprovoked disciplinary action.

I remember a few drill instructors (DIs) who were really tough. It seemed that the army authorities looked for weaknesses in every new soldier's file and then devised activities to drive them to quit. I remember one guy who fell asleep during training, and the DIs picked on him heavily. They made me low crawl (crawl as close to the ground as possible for long periods of time to avoid detection) more than anybody in my platoon, but I would not quit. I'm not sure where my resolve came from, but I wanted to prove to myself that even under extreme pressure, I would not quit. Two of my fellow soldiers must have decided it was too hard for them, though, because they went absent without leave (AWOL). One of them was caught and paraded in front of us, just to let us know the seriousness of the consequences.

As a Christian today, I know Satan also looks for our weaknesses and tries to capitalize on them. Just as I refused to give in to the army authorities who were targeting me and trying to make me quit, now as a Christian, I stand firm and refuse to give in to Satan's attempts to capitalize on my weaknesses.

After my basic training in Fork Polk, I traveled to Texas for my Advanced Individual Training (AIT), where I received two months of training in Hawk Missiles. I was then sent to Germany, where I was in a missile battalion and tasked with putting missiles on top of launchers. After three weeks, they threw me out of the missile outfit and put me in a tank division because they learned that I had recently applied to go to Vietnam. After the transfer, I trained on tanks for seven months. Altogether, I was in the military for about eleven months before I turned eighteen and was finally able to go fight in a very unpopular war in Vietnam.

My daddy fought in World War II, and he had told me about his exploits in Guadalcanal against the Japanese. My time in Germany wasn't what I'd envisioned of the army, and it didn't sound like my daddy's time in the military, so I put in a 1049 application to go to Vietnam. I like action and adventure, and that wasn't going on in Germany. I wanted to experience combat. Plus, Germany was cold!

When I think of all our military who fought in Vietnam and who have fought for our country since its beginning, my mind goes to the Lord Jesus and all He did for us. After I became a Christian, I learned what Jesus the Christ did for me and for all mankind. We, as Americans in the armed forces, do it for our country and loved ones. Jesus did it for even the ones who were putting him to death. He said on the cross, "Father, forgive them; for they know not what they do" (Luke 23:34). John 15:13 says, "Greater love hath no man than this, that a man lay down his life for his friends." The Lord of glory laid down His life for the whole world. He took upon Himself the sins of the whole world—past, present, and future.

Nothing compares with Jesus laying down His life for the whole world. The sacrifice of nearly 60,000[1] American soldiers who died in Vietnam makes me appreciate, however, even more what Jesus Christ did for us 2,000 years ago. I had no concept of the Lord's sacrifice while I was serving, though, and no idea of how God would help me make peace with my experiences.

I was wounded in Vietnam, and my best friend lost his life there. After I came to the Lord Jesus, I began asking Him questions about Vietnam. The Lord said to me, "I sent you there to learn war." *Sent* is an interesting word. When the Lord sends someone, there is apostolic meaning to it. For example, in John 6:44, Jesus says, "No man can come to me, except the Father which hath sent me draw him: and I will raise him up at the last day." And in Hebrews 3:1, we see that God sent Jesus as an apostle. He also sent apostles throughout the New Testament. Acts 13:4 informs us that the Holy Ghost sent Paul and Barnabas on their travels to spread the news of Jesus. Since we know that these two men were known as apostles

(Acts 14:4), we see here the special apostolic, anointed, powerful release given to Jesus and these men when they were *sent* out by Father God and Holy Ghost.

Though I, of course, was not given the same mission or anointing as Christ, Paul, Barnabas, or any of the other apostles of the New Testament, God had a specific, anointed purpose in sending me to Vietnam.

★ ★ CHAPTER 2

FIGHT THE GOOD FIGHT

Put on the whole armour of God, that ye may be able to stand against the wiles of the devil.

Ephesians 6:11

GOD SENT ME TO VIETNAM so I could one day be a spiritual warrior. So many things happened in Vietnam that Father God wanted me to experience and relate to Christianity. As the body of Christ Jesus, we cannot allow ourselves to stop being in war. We are in war not with M-16 rifles or 50-calibre machine guns, but war, nevertheless.

As warriors, we must "fight the good fight of faith." As the apostle Paul declares in 1 Timothy 6:12, we must fight this war by faith. And Hebrews 12:2 states, "Looking unto Jesus the author and finisher of our faith."

Experiential knowledge is so essential in the body of Christ. Warfare in the natural helps in understanding spiritual warfare. The Bible tells us the natural comes before the spiritual. The apostle Paul writes in 1 Corinthians 15:45–47, "The first man Adam was made a living soul; the last Adam was made a quickening spirit. Howbeit that was not first which is spiritual, but that which is natural; and afterward that which is spiritual. The first man is of the earth, earthy; the second man is the Lord from heaven."

What exactly is spiritual warfare? Spiritual warfare is war in the unseen, invisible world waged by the ultimate Enemy, Satan. The devil is in opposition to God and doesn't want God to be glorified. He doesn't want you to grow in your faith. He doesn't want you to share your faith with others. He doesn't want others to come to know Jesus. He doesn't want a world of grace, mercy, forgiveness, love, kindness, joy, and peace. He is at work with evil forces so that those things don't happen. How does the Bible describe God? God is described as love (1 John 4:8); as the way, the truth, and the life (John 14:6); as holy (1 Samuel 2:2); as Comforter (John 14:26); as our shepherd (Psalm 23:1); as our helper (Hebrews 13:6); and the list could go on. Satan is anything opposite. But he is deceitful and uses his lies and deception to tempt us away from God and to make things appear as if they are from God. We must be on the lookout for him and for his lies.

In physical war, there are many dangers that take place with military persons, particularly combat personnel. Combat people are in harm's way almost all the time and have to always be aware of attack from the enemy. Christians are under constant attack from the devil as well. Jesus said in John 10:10, "The thief cometh not, but for to steal, and to kill, and to destroy: I am come that they might have life, and that they might have it more abundantly." Notice the thief comes at night when we are least expecting him. The correlation is evident between physical and natural warfare and Satan's war against Christians.

Vietnam fighters are known and were known for their guerrilla warfare. The Vietcong would attack when least expected. The North Vietnamese Army (NVA) is the regular army from North Vietnam; the Vietcong (VC or Charlie) were loosely organized, mostly untrained groups of guerrilla fighters not belonging to the North Vietnamese military who operated primarily in South Vietnam. Most of the time when in Vietnam, we were attacked at night in South, short for Southern Vietnam. I like to call the Vietcong "the pajama boys wearing black pajamas—but a great deal more effective." Of course the VC and NVA weren't Satan, but they illustrate how the Enemy attacks when least expected.

In the Vietnam War, we had to be hypervigilant—always looking for something to take place and always being on the alert. The devil is our adversary and on the lookout for whom to devour (1 Peter 5:8). He wants to devour us. As Christians we must know that this is a war. We belong to Christ and need to be on alert always.

When in Vietnam, I had to pull guard, or watch for at least two hours a shift. But it was not just on guard duty that I would watch. We were always on alert, ever watching for an attack. We fought an elusive enemy who often blended in with the rest of the Vietnamese. Charlie could have been a young teenage boy or girl with explosives strapped to their body. It made no difference to the Vietcong. So it is with Satan; nobody is off limits. Even while in Germany in 1966, I had to pull guard. Russia was always threatening. We had to challenge many people who came through the gate for identification, ensuring that everyone we allowed in was supposed to be there. One mess-up could be costly.

Satan is elusive, hard to spot, and easily blends in with our surroundings, disguising himself as an apostle of Christ. "For such are false apostles, deceitful workers, transforming themselves into the apostles of Christ. And no marvel; for Satan himself is transformed into an angel of light" (2 Corinthians 11:13–14).

If we let our guards down as Christians, we can let Satan worm his way in without knowing what hit us. The devil hates Christians. Beloved, I say it again: it is war. The Bible says that the joy of the Lord is our strength, and we need to contend for the faith—that is, fight.

Jude verse 3 states, "Beloved, when I gave all diligence to write unto you of the common salvation, it was needful for me to write unto you, and exhort you that ye should earnestly contend for the faith which was once delivered unto the saints."

If a Christian thinks he or she is not in a spiritual war, that person is sadly mistaken; the devil is poised and ready to pounce.

As the body of Christ Jesus, we cannot allow ourselves to stop being in war.

Our weapons against Satan aren't fists or 45-calibre pistols, but they are powerful weapons. Second Corinthians 10:4 states, "(For the weapons of our warfare are not carnal, but mighty through God to the pulling down of strongholds.)"

When I think of strongholds, I think of the strongholds in Vietnam, particularly in North Vietnam. We were not supposed to go there, and it was a demilitarized zone (DMZ). However, both the NVA's forces and our forces entered the DMZ all the time. With spiritual weapons, we can knock down any strongholds that keep people from God.

But we can't knock down strongholds by using our armor and weapons during wartime without training and practice. We must know how to use our defensive and offensive weapons and have them ready at all times. Military personnel receive training *before* they go to war, so they know how to fight. And in war, soldiers don't wait to pick up their weapons until the battle begins—that would be disastrous. Brothers and Sisters in Christ, grow strong in the Lord, and be on alert with your spiritual weapons and armor.

Armor of God

As I explained in the introduction, the Bible makes clear that attacks from Satan are inevitable, so we must be prepared for them. However, the Bible helps us to be properly equipped for those attacks, both for keeping Satan from stealing from us and to empower us to advance and take ground from him. Thankfully, we are not left to fight this battle alone!

> Finally, my brethren, be strong in the Lord, and in the power of his might. Put on the whole armour of God, that ye may be able to stand against the wiles of the devil. For we wrestle not against flesh and blood, but against principalities, against powers, against the rulers of the darkness of this world, against

> spiritual wickedness in high places. Wherefore take unto you the whole armour of God, that ye may be able to withstand in the evil day, and having done all, to stand. Stand therefore, having your loins girt about with truth, and having on the breastplate of righteousness; And your feet shod with the preparation of the gospel of peace; Above all, taking the shield of faith, wherewith ye shall be able to quench all the fiery darts of the wicked. And take the helmet of salvation, and the sword of the Spirit, which is the word of God: Praying always with all prayer and supplication in the Spirit, and watching thereunto with all perseverance and supplication for all saints. (Ephesians 6:10–18)

Warriors in Roman days wore belts, which were essential to protect their loins and hold their weapons, ropes, and food rations.[2] So in Paul's letter to the Ephesians, we learn the importance of having "your loins girt about with truth," or as the NIV version says, "Stand firm with the belt of truth buckled around your waist." What does that mean? It is an analogy for God's truth. Jesus describes Himself as "the truth," in John 14:6. We can fight off the devil by knowing Jesus and by knowing the truth found only in the Bible. His truth needs to encircle us like a belt so we do not fall prey to Satan's lies. By knowing God's truth, we can more easily know right from wrong, fight temptation, and spot lies and things in opposition to God.

Next, we are to put on the "breastplate of righteousness." The breastplate is a key part of armor because it protects a warrior's vital organs, which represent our minds and emotions.[3] For Christians, this means striving for the righteousness and perfection of God and not striving for the calls of the world or living lives dictated by sin. Though we will never achieve the perfect righteousness of God, it should be our aim.[4]

Paul then instructs us to ensure that our feet are "shod with the preparation of the gospel of peace." In Bible times, warriors' shoes had spikes on the bottom, similar to cleats, to help them navigate rough terrain and keep a solid foundation for traveling. In the army, we wore jungle boots. With a solid footing, we can maintain peace and withstand obstacles when Satan tries to interfere with our relationship with God and with others. With solid footing, we can spread God's message of peace to others.[5]

Paul says, "Above all, taking the shield of faith." Fiery arrows were used as weapons, and shields were indispensable in blocking and extinguishing them. Additionally, shields could be used to push back against the enemy.[6] Without faith, we cannot fight off our Enemy. What is faith? Faith is not merely believing, but also trusting despite our inability to see. "Now faith is the substance of things hoped for, the evidence of things not seen" (Hebrews 11:1).

The helmet of salvation represents salvation itself. In the Bible, the head represented the entire person. In the army, we wore steel helmets for protection. In the days of Paul, helmets varied quite a bit. Some were made of metal, and some were made of leather with metal reinforcements. Helmets usually had cheek and neck protection. Regardless of the differences in helmets, they were all designed to protect from deadly hits to the head.[7] Without salvation, we are spiritually dead. We are to daily keep our hope in the confidence of our salvation in Jesus to protect any darts of doubt that Satan throws at us. And how do we receive that salvation? By believing God gave His Son Jesus as the Savior to this world, that He died on a cross for our sins, rose from the grave, and now sits at the right hand of God the Father in Heaven. By believing and trusting in that, and by asking to receive Jesus as our Savior, we get the privilege to be with Him in heaven one day, despite our sins.[8]

The sword of the Spirit, which represents God's Word, the Bible, is the only offensive weapon. By reading the Bible and memorizing Scripture, we have quick access to His truths to help combat the Enemy. Reading the Bible and knowing Scripture is a huge part of my life. More to come in chapter 5 about that.

Lastly, Paul tells us to pray always. There is mighty power in prayer. Power to know the will of God. Power to fight off evil, darkness, and temptation. Power to heal. Power to receive wisdom. Power to receive mercy and forgiveness. Power to receive help. Power to know our Savior. I will speak more about prayer in chapter 5 as well.

If Father God chose you, you will become a soldier and a warrior. Being a warrior in the Spirit is far greater than being a natural warrior. There are many spiritual beings that need to be dealt with. But the way we fight in God is by the Spirit and with His armor. Take heart that He is omnipresent, omniscient, and omnipotent. Satan is not.

Since the beginning, Father God has been working to bring the whole world to salvation and to come into His kingdom. We are promised ultimate victory from Isaiah 54:17, which declares, "No weapon that is formed against thee shall prosper; and every tongue that shall rise against thee in judgment thou shalt condemn. This is the heritage of the servants of the LORD, and their righteousness is of me, saith the LORD."

We did not win the war in Vietnam. But in the war between good and evil, light and darkness, God and Satan, God wins.

★ ★ CHAPTER 3

MEETING GOD AND REALIZING MY GIFTS

And he gave some, apostles; and some, prophets; and some, evangelists; and some, pastors and teachers.

Ephesians 4:11

AFTER I RETURNED FROM VIETNAM, I succumbed to drunkenness and drug abuse, but I didn't want to live that way. Even though I didn't really know God, I started crying out to Him, that He would take those things away from me. Most of the churches in Rayne, Louisiana, were Catholic churches. Two different times I went inside the church between mass services to ask God for help. One time I was so drunk and high that I hiked myself over the rails to the place where the priests and altar boys hung out, fell asleep, and got some good z's. There was no instantaneous change though.

God was slowly drawing me into His kingdom. Two years after falling asleep at the church, I went to a guy's house with my buddy after playing softball. The guy, Emory Menard, preached Jesus. I knew right then on that September day in 1975 that the Holy Ghost came upon me and sealed my spirit. I learned that whenever God draws you into His kingdom, you are marked. I was a dirtbag sinner. But God cleans those whom He wants as His people. I refer to my time before coming to Christ as BC, "Before Christ." Everyone who comes to Jesus has a "Before Christ." We all must call upon Jesus individually. No one can do it for us. God must draw us first. Jesus said in John 6:44, "No man can come to me, except the Father which hath sent me draw him: and I will raise him up at the last day."

My beautiful girlfriend at the time, Sheila, was with me that day and also decided to follow Jesus after hearing the gospel. We were married in November and have spent our entire marriage following Jesus and growing together in our faith.

In the military, I got my orders from my commanding officer. I now get my orders from God. As a new Christian, I started small with learning God's Word. New soldiers start off small—nobody promotes to a general overnight. The Bible says not to despise small beginnings: "For who hath despised the day of small things? for they shall rejoice, and shall see the plummet in the hand of Zerubbabel with those seven; they are the eyes of the Lord, which run to and fro through the whole earth" (Zechariah 4:10). Regardless of rank, however, all positions in the military and Christianity are important and play a role in the mission.

Appointed by God

In the US Army, there are generals, colonels, majors, captains, and lieutenants. There are commissioned and noncommissioned officers and privates. The highest rank that I achieved during my time in the army was E-5, Specialist Fifth Class. In the army of the Lord, there are officers as well: apostles, prophets, evangelists, pastors, and teachers (Ephesians 4:11). Believers who are called to one of these ministries are known as fivefold officers. Officers in the military earn their ranks, but the Lord gives gifts to equip His officers. Five is the number of grace (Companion Bible, appendix 10, p. 14). Grace is always needed. To experience these gifts, you must first be born again. Further, you must be baptized in the Holy Ghost.

The Lord has given me gifts and called me as a fivefold office prophet and seer of Him. When I say that I am a called prophet and seer, I mean that God has spoken through prophetic ministers to declare to me that God has called me to minister to others as His prophet and seer, but it also means that I have not yet been ordained as a prophet or seer by Christian leaders appointed for that purpose. But if you're like I was, you've never heard of a prophet or seer of God. I compare prophets and seers to point men in the military.

In Vietnam, we would go on foot patrols in the jungle. Most times, I was the point man. A point man walks about five yards ahead of the squad and the squad leader. The squad leader would be in the middle of the column next to the radio man. Moreover, the squad leader had to be protected because he knew how to call in coordinates if we got into trouble—if Charlie attacked. But we never got attacked when on foot patrols. Once while on a foot patrol when I was the point man, we were getting ready to ford a stream. I sank in mud up to my knees and had to be hauled out by two men who were on patrol with me.

Samuel in the Bible was a prophet and a seer. As a boy, he began receiving messages from God. The people of Israel recognized his authority and consulted with him.

The story of Ishmael, Abraham's son, is another example of prophecy in the Bible. Hagar was Ishmael's mother. According to Genesis 16:12, an angel of the Lord prophesied to Hagar about Ishmael: "And he will be a wild man; his hand will be against every man, and every man's hand against him; and he shall dwell in the presence of all his brethren." Hagar was Egyptian, and every man's hand was against her son, Ishmael, and vice versa. But God is still on His throne, and He always knows what He is doing. He controls the universe, and the earth is His footstool. Sarai should have waited for her son, Isaac, to be born and for the promise to come to pass. However, she wanted a child *now*. But we must all wait. Isaiah 40:31 says, "But they that wait upon the LORD shall renew their strength; they shall mount up with wings as eagles; they shall run, and not be weary; and they shall walk, and not be faint."

I believe that in the body of Christ, the point men and women are the prophets and seers, with the job of seeing and watching. Both my wife and I see and watch as called prophets of the living God. Prophets are charged with speaking the word of the Lord that Holy Ghost gives us, words that we hear Him say to us. I am also a seer. Seers are given visions from God and are to speak those visions. In 2006, one of our former pastors called me a seer by the Spirit of the living God. When he prophesied this to me, I had to look up the term *seer* for myself.

Paul tells us in Ephesians 2:20 that the household of God is "built upon the foundation of the apostles and prophets, Jesus Christ himself being the chief corner stone." Apostles, prophets, and seers are all foundational ministers. They are point men and women who see ahead for the body of Christ. Officers of the Lord are designed to equip the other soldiers. As a called prophet, God has given me a gift to help fellow Christians.

I believe that seers and prophets are so needed in the kingdom of the living God, more so today than ever before. Prophecy is a weapon to destroy the works of the devil and to bring help and healing to others. It is the word of the Lord! As prophets, we hear what the Lord says, and we speak the truth, whatever He says.

Revelation 19:10 says, "For the testimony of Jesus is the spirit of prophecy." Second Peter 1:21 explains, "For the prophecy came not in old time by the will of man: but holy men of God spake as they were moved by the Holy Ghost." Holy Ghost still moves today. We have so many wonderful weapons. Also, 2 Peter 1:19 declares, "We have also a more sure word of prophecy; whereunto ye do well that ye take heed, as unto a light that shineth in a dark place, until the day dawn, and the day star arise in your hearts."

God uses prophets to assist in building His church from the foundational level. He uses His prophets to both preach and give prophetic words of truth from the Bible to strengthen and instruct God's people and leaders. Prophets share and speak words of encouragement or inspiration to church leaders who are struggling, words of warning or correction to churches who are straying from the Lord and are trying to become like the world, words of wisdom to aid in difficult decision-making, words of affirmation for those whom the Lord wants to commend for their unwavering faithfulness to Him, and myriad other messages that help create a firm foundation for the body of Christ.

In addition to using prophets to build up the church as a whole, God uses prophets to minister to individuals. Paul illustrates the power of this ministry in 1 Corinthians 14:24–25, where God can use prophecy to expose the heart of an unbeliever who attends a church gathering to the point where that person would worship God and know that God's presence is among the people of that church. But God also uses His prophets to prophesy to His children individually. One way in which God does this is by having a prophet minister hope-filled, healing words to a believer concerning a particular hardship in that believer's life to encourage and strengthen that person by showing him or her that the Lord truly cares about the distress in that person's life and that He will see him or her through it. Further, God sometimes uses prophecy to bring direction for ministry for someone who has been privately praying for an answer from the Lord in that area. The Lord will also use prophecy to give directives to an individual to study certain Scriptures, to prepare for intensive spiritual warfare that is upcoming, or to focus more specifically on certain attributes of God to strengthen that person's trust in the Lord. When God uses His prophets, it is always to build people up, even when the directives are for His people to change their ways in certain areas of life. So if prophets are not utilized in the body of Christ, their critical and unique gifts to build His church are wasted, and the building process is greatly hampered.

Trained in the Lord

As new Christians, my wife and I started at a church and stayed there for eight years. Wanting to grow in our faith more, however, Sheila and I moved to a new church where we learned about the spiritual gifts God gives, including prophecy. I believe God stations Christians at different churches. Our base camp (church) today is in Baton Rouge. When I was in Vietnam, I was stationed at Bear Cat. God places us where we can best be used.

At our new church, we began prayer meetings where we witnessed people seeing visions and casting out demons. This new church also opened the doors for me to begin learning about and being trained in prophetic ministry. I began prophesying to people even before I knew much about prophetic ministry. If I received a message or vision from the Lord for someone, I simply walked up to that person and gave the message without understanding that I was prophesying to that person. It was encouraging that most people were blessed by the prophetic words the Lord spoke through me to them.

In 1989, the pastor at our new church, who was an ordained prophetic pastor, taught us about prophetic ministry. My wife and I learned that all Christians can operate in the gift of prophesying, while there are some whom God calls to the office of prophet. In other words, God may anoint someone to occasionally minister a prophetic message, but He gives special anointing to those He calls to be prophets. It is the same with all of the gifts—He can anoint all believers to minister through all the spiritual gifts at times, but He calls some believers to minister uniquely and expertly in a few specific gifts.

God told me He was calling me to be a prophet. I began attending training sessions and conferences to sharpen my prophetic gifts to prophesy more clearly, accurately, and effectively. I was placed in various scenarios where I would have to rely on the Lord to give a prophetic message. Afterward, the recipient was asked if the prophetic word had been accurate. I already had a strong anointing for boldly ministering prophetic messages to others, so ministering in these scenarios was not fearful for me. God used these trainings to sharpen my prophetic gifts.

I also received instruction regarding the etiquette of prophesying to others, such as best practices in ministering prophetic words that contained very private information or a strong message of correction. Additionally, I was taught not to allow the blessing of my gifts to supersede the importance of striving by the Spirit to improve godly character, not to be prideful about my gifts, and to walk in humility when ministering. "Pride goeth before destruction, and an haughty spirit before a fall" (Proverbs 16:18).

Though I've had training, I am qualified not by man's standards, but by God's standards. He calls and never repents of His gifts and callings. He is the one who qualified me and many others. It is about Him. First Samuel 2:6–7 says, "The Lord killeth, and maketh alive: he bringeth down to the grave, and bringeth up. The Lord maketh poor, and maketh rich: he bringeth low, and lifteth up."

Where my wife and I currently fellowship, I have an apostle that I am under who watches as well. I feel like the Roman soldier who went to Jesus for the healing of his servant, and Jesus said, "I will come." The soldier replied, "It is not necessary. I have authority and am under authority." Though I as a called prophet have God-given authority, I must submit under my apostle's authority. And, most importantly, I must submit to God.

Though I am an officer in God's army, promotion comes extremely slow. Advancement does not come overnight in the US Army, but it comes much quicker when compared to promotion in the Lord's army.

I knew a man in Vietnam who would "brownnose" or play up to people in charge for promotion, which was unethical. We need to do our jobs. The Bible says, "For promotion cometh neither from the east nor from the west, nor from the south. But God is the judge: he putteth down one, and setteth up another" (Psalm 75:6–7).

It reminds me of the time I was in Vietnam and was threatened with a court-martial. I had an armful of dud mortar rounds, and my captain told me to drop what I was doing and get my helmet and flak jacket on. I told him, "You are crazy!" He said, "I am going to have you court-martialed." Three days later, I was wounded and got promoted—without brownnosing.

Holy Ghost gave me a vision about three years ago. In the vision was a totem pole in my living room while I was watching television. The Spirit of the Living God had the audacity to interrupt my television watching! I was at the bottom of the pole yet still on the pole. As a warrior in Vietnam, I was impressed with the men I fought with. One received a Silver Star. The men I fought with were brave men, including my best friend. For me, any man or woman who goes to war for this country is brave. I salute them. It is about the Lord and whom He chooses. He chose me to be in His kingdom as well as many others. He chose me to be His seer and prophet along with others, but I'm a low man on the totem pole. Praise the name of the Lord!

Submission

God provided me with gifts, but I had to learn spiritual submission before I realized my gifts. Though I should have learned about submitting to authority in the military, I'm a stubborn guy, and it took me a long time to learn about submission.

Six months after I was born again, Father God gave me a vision. In the vision, I was preaching at the train depot lot in Rayne, Louisiana, to about fifteen or twenty people, with a passenger train passing through going from east to west. Then, thirty years after the vision, my wife and I became ordained ministers after Father God sent me to be trained at Rhema Bible Training Center in Broken Arrow, Oklahoma. Praise the Lord!

The primary reason for the thirty-year delay was because I had to learn to submit to authority, especially spiritual authority. For me, submission is hard-core training. You would think I would have had enough training in this area in the US Army. In Vietnam, I was not a good soldier. Good soldiers take orders and follow through with them. Taking orders has never been a strong suit of mine.

I had to learn to submit to the Most High God, which in itself is big-time stuff. I had to believe that I heard His voice, and I had to believe His written Word. To submit to these two elements, to God and to people in authority, is quite a difficult process.

We are so blessed at our church, as we have many prophetic people there, seers with prophetic anointing. What an army God has! Jesus is the Lord Sabaoth. In Romans 9:29, Paul talked about God leaving us a seed (descendants). Sabaoth means army. What a God we serve!

The Lord Jesus is the Commander in Chief of His army, and in every part of His army. He is over all. Colossians 1:18 says, "And he is the head of the body, the church: who is the beginning, the firstborn from the dead; that in all things he might have the preeminence." Similarly, Ephesians 1:22 states, "And hath put all things under his feet, and gave him to be the head over all things to the church." That is our Jesus; He is the Christ, the head of the church.

★ ★ CHAPTER 4

EQUIPPING, ENCOURAGING, AND HELPING IN TRUTH

The Spirit of the Lord GOD is upon me; because the LORD hath anointed me to preach good tidings unto the meek; he hath sent me to bind up the brokenhearted, to proclaim liberty to the captives, and the opening of the prison to them that are bound.

Isaiah 61:1

NOW THAT I AM AN officer in God's kingdom, my job is to equip others to do the work of the ministry; I teach, preach, and prophesy. Officers and noncommissioned officers (NCOs) do the same thing in the United States Army by equipping those in their charge.

Father God wanted me to go through war to learn, experience, and tell about it. This is the fight: to be wounded both physically and emotionally and tell about it. As a called prophet and seer, I want the body of Christ to be healed emotionally, spiritually, and mentally. The prophet has the ability, along with many others, to aid hurting people in the healing process. But it must be done in truth. Remember Jesus is the Truth. No one else holds that title. The truth is the center of who Jesus is. It is revelation of God's Word. "Jesus saith unto him, I am the way, the truth, and the life: no man cometh unto the Father, but by me" (John 14:6). As God's body, we cannot do without the truth. We need to hear the truth from prophets and fivefold ministers. Speak the truth in love (Ephesians 4:15).

I'm always listening so I know if God wants me to help someone. While I'm grocery shopping, I may hear the Holy Spirit tell me to go tell someone that God loves them, so I do. Sometimes I get a picture that comes to me, and the Lord will enhance that picture, or I may just have an impression in my spirit. If the Lord tells me to lay hands on someone, I will get a picture that may go way back to that person's childhood, and I may receive a word of knowledge to help that person heal. Sometimes when I lay hands on someone, I can feel every hurt and every pain they've been through. Then I share with them, and the Lord starts healing their physical and emotional wounds. I once laid hands on someone, and I told her that I sensed from God that she had some issues with her female organs. She began crying, telling me she'd had an abortion. She was able to accept God's forgiveness and delivery from her sin.

The Lord Jesus always spoke the truth while He walked this earth because He is the Truth. And remember, truth is the belt of righteousness.

I believe the Lord sends in a prophet, and at times an apostle, to rip the bandages off wounds and start to repair. During my medical treatment after being wounded in Vietnam, I had bandages on my forearms, and it felt like they were ripping the whole inside out of my arm every time they had to rip them off to change them. Repair work on our souls can be painful too.

Prophets and apostles can rip off bandages and start the healing process. The wounds need repair, but the bandages must come off first. This process hurts a great deal, and for me, it hurt. God is the surgeon. Prophets hear what God is saying. Many people blame the messenger, but if they would hear the prophet, they would recover. I am talking about true prophets, not false prophets. False prophets in old covenant days spoke of peace when God said no peace. A true prophet will speak only what the Lord tells that prophet to speak.

When we get wounded, the bandages must come off, and we need to be overcomers by the Word of the Living God in truth by our faith. If you are in the faith, you want to hear the truth. The ministry my wife and I have in which we prophecy and encourage is called Truth Ministries because we speak the truth. God had to do a remarkable thing in us. First, He had to recreate us. And that is exactly what God the Father did in Jesus the Son. First the way, then the truth, and finally the life. What a God we serve! Today, I am a son of the living God because of Jesus. John 1:12 says, "But as many as received him, to them gave he power to become the sons of God, even to them that believe on his name." What power we have in and from Jesus.

God wants us to speak the truth in love, even when it's hard. Ephesians 4:15 says, "But speaking the truth in love, may grow up into Him in all things, which is the Head, even Christ." It is a war—a great war. With this war, we could lose our spirit, soul, and body. One of our pastors used to put 1 Thessalonians 5:23 this way: "We are spirit, we have a soul, and we live in a body." So speak the truth in love.

As a called seer and prophet of God, I have helped many people come to know God, hear hard truths, and experience physical and emotional healing. There are many times when people have come to Sheila and me for counsel, and the Lord has urged us to lovingly expose sin in their lives, urge them to change, and give them practical solutions to begin that change. However, there are also times when Sheila and I have had to take the initiative to confront people, especially believers, who have refused to face their sin or to do anything about it. These confrontations can be difficult, but the Lord has stood by us and helped us to remain unmovable in our resolve to bring the truth to bear. As we have grown in experiencing Jesus's love, we have improved our ability to speak His truth in love to those who have strayed from Him.

It is a privilege to be able to provide a word of encouragement to people. Recently Holy Ghost came upon me concerning a woman we know who works near our home. I saw in a vision this woman sweeping with a broom. Holy Ghost said, "Go and prophesy to her." I went to help as God's called prophet by giving her an encouraging word: the Lord was using her to help clean dirt from people's lives. She was very encouraged and told me that she and her mother were urging her sister to change her lifestyle. God confirmed with a prophetic word to encourage her in that difficult time with her sister. We serve a great God. She explained what was going on and wept. Through my vision from the Lord, she was encouraged to persevere with her sister.

Remember friends, your words can be so encouraging to people, whether you are a prophet or not. When in Vietnam, I had a friend who was going through a rough time and wanted to quit. I was summoned by my platoon leader to talk to my friend. I had been in Vietnam a long time—about nine months—and I knew the score. I encouraged him to keep going: "Pick yourself up by your boot strings and get on the ball. Your time is almost up. You can't quit now." Thankfully, my urgings helped him because he did not quit and survived to tell about it. It was my goal to help my buddy in Vietnam. Today, a greater anointing is upon me to help.

One of our goals as lovers of Jesus should be to help people. It is vitally important that we, as Christians, help one another. We must learn to pray and ask the Lord first to find out what is going on with that person. He may simply want us to pray in the name of Jesus. God is sovereign over all. But when Holy Ghost comes upon us to give, to help, then we give, we help.

Be on the lookout to help and encourage. We look at our brothers and sisters in the Lord and watch to see if they are hurting physically or mentally and ask if they need prayer. We are on alert, watching, as watchmen on the wall. Ezekiel 33:6 states, "But if the watchman see the sword come, and blow not the trumpet, and the people be not warned; if the sword come, and take any person from among them, he is taken away in his iniquity; but his blood will I require at the watchman's hand."

Whatever our calling, God wants us to help people with whatever gifts we have. In Vietnam, there was a medic whom I will call Doc, a conscientious objector from Georgia. He talked about his relationship with Jesus constantly. At the time that I knew Doc, it was "Before Christ"—BC for me. However, during my time knowing Doc, I experienced an extraordinary event involving him. We were sweeping for mines on a trail in the jungle when a mine went off. A man sweeping was injured. Doc jumped out of the track with no weapons at all and looked after the injured man. Now, in my book, a man like Doc will go far. We need men like that in this country—men, regardless of their convictions, who will "fight the good fight of faith."

Another incident took place the day my best friend was killed and I was wounded. I saw one of our mechanics carrying a wounded soldier to safety, who was allied with the Army of the Republic of Vietnam (ARVN) soldiers. We are all trained to fight, but helping another soldier from a different army—that is Christlike.

After I was wounded, the doctors and nurses administered tremendous care to me until I reached full recovery. They used their God-given gifts to provide care, comfort, and compassion for me. I want to thank all the physicians, nurses, and medics who helped all of us. I have sincere thankfulness to all medical personnel who serve soldiers now and in all past conflicts. Without them and the Lord, warriors cannot heal. We all work together.

Helping can come in so many forms. It can mean just lifting somebody's spirits. My best friend, Patrick, did that for me in Vietnam after I was recovering from malaria and also experiencing seasickness. We took a ship from Saigon to Da Nang, Vietnam, on the South China Sea. I remained seasick the entire four days. Patrick would come around and tease me with a mess kit of rice, knowing I could not eat due to the seasickness. At the end of the trip, we anchored the ship in Da Nang Harbor. He said, "Let's jump ship, Don!" And we did. He jumped from the ship's bow; then I jumped. He swam all around the ship. I could not do that, as I had just gotten out of the hospital after treatment for malaria. I could only swim to the front of the ship, barely making it up the ladder, where I collapsed on the deck. On the other hand, my friend made a swan dive off the bow. I needed my spirits lifted, and this simple gesture was encouraging. Look to do the same for your friends.

Helping can mean being supportive of one another. When I was made track commander with no qualifications, I was soon replaced by a staff sergeant who came to our troop. I had no bad feelings about that. The staff sergeant didn't know anything about cavalry tactics, since he'd come from infantry, and he knew nothing about cleaning a 50-calibre machine gun, so I helped him, and we got along great.

It's the same in the body of Christ. We aren't to be jealous of one another's gifts and experiences; we should support one another and work together. The Bible says we all work together for the good of God. "From whom the whole body fitly joined together and compacted by that which every joint supplieth, according to the effectual working in the measure of every part, maketh increase of the body unto the edifying of itself in love" (Ephesians 4:16).

When I was recovering from my war wounds in the hospital, the entertainer, Bob Hope, came to San Antonio to the River Parade. They brought all those who were ambulatory to the parade so we could see him. Bob Hope used his gifts to lift our spirits. I don't know if Bob Hope was a Christian, but think of how much more we as Christians can do to help our friends.

★ ★ CHAPTER 5

NOURISHMENT FOR STAYING STRONG

And Jesus said unto them, I am the bread of life: he that cometh to me shall never hunger; and he that believeth on me shall never thirst.
John 6:35

AFTER I MET AND ACCEPTED Jesus in September 1975, I began to crave Him like a craved food—I craved spending time with Him, craved learning about Him, craved getting to know Him. And I know a lot about cravings from my time in Vietnam.

The cultural eats in Cajun country are delicious, and while I was serving, I sure missed good Cajun gumbo as well as both meatball and chicken fricassee. The first lieutenant I met in Vietnam was my platoon leader, and he was from California. He craved McDonald's hamburgers and frequently talked about them. I'd never even heard of McDonald's but would have loved a good hamburger from the mom-and-pop drive-ins back in Rayne.

In Vietnam we ate C rations, which came in a can and contained meals such as beans and wieners, meatballs and beans, or beefsteak—all nasty-tasting stuff, but it sustained us. We often used C-4 for cooking. C-4 was an explosive that we used to blow up things, but it came in handy for cooking. It came in a block, and we'd take a piece of C-4, put it in the lock hole of a cargo hatch of a track, light it, set a steel pot or even a helmet full of the nasty canned food on top of the C-4, and let it cook. Voila, your meal for the day! I got my hands on some Louisiana Brand Hot Sauce™ once and tried to recreate the tastes of home, but all it did was tear up the stomach of my staff sergeant, which he wasn't too happy about. Oh, how I craved a home-cooked meal, but the C rations did their job and sustained us with energy.

Spiritual food is much greater than even the best home-cooked dinner or fancy restaurant meal. Jesus said in Matthew 5:6, "Blessed are they which do hunger and thirst after righteousness: for they shall be filled." Even more than the deep cravings I had for some good Cajun food, we should all crave the holiness and righteousness of God.

Certain food used to be restricted in the Old Testament. Before Jesus came to earth, followers of God had to follow certain rules, including certain rules with food. The coming of Jesus abolished these types of Old Testament laws. "For the kingdom of God is not meat and drink; but righteousness, and peace, and joy in the Holy Ghost" (Romans 14:17). There is such beauty that the God of the Old Testament is the same as the God of the New Testament. He is the same yesterday, today, and forever (Hebrews 13:8).

Because Jesus died for us, we no longer need to follow rules about food, circumcision, animal sacrifices, or other ceremonial laws to go to heaven. That was the way of the Old Covenant. Jesus bridged the gap for us. The Bible says, "For God so loved the world that he gave his one and only Son, that whoever believes in him shall not perish but have eternal life" (John 3:16 NIV). This is my favorite verse in the Bible. Despite our sins and blunders, we can still follow Jesus and meet and reign with Him as He brings the fullness of heaven to earth someday. There are no restrictions in coming to Him—we only need to believe, obey, and love Him.

"And Jesus said to them, 'I am the bread of life. He who comes to Me shall never hunger, and he who believes in Me shall never thirst'" (John 6:35 NKJV). Unlike physical food and drink, Jesus is not a temporary answer to quench our needs; He is life-giving. We need Him for spiritual survival.

As natural food sustains us with energy to live our daily lives, spiritual food sustains us to fight off Satan and his temptations. I cannot emphasize enough that prayer and the Bible are our offensive spiritual weapons, our spiritual food, the key to staying connected to God and to standing strong against Satan. Reading the Bible and praying provide us with spiritual sustenance to live our lives as followers of Him and to fight off Satan's temptations. When Jesus spent time in the wilderness, He went without food. He was physically weak but spiritually strong. He knew His Father. And with every temptation Satan threw at Jesus, Jesus answered with His Father's words.

The Word of God

The Bible is God's own words to us. It enables us to know Him and His ways. Second Timothy 3:16 says, "All scripture is given by inspiration of God, and is profitable for doctrine, for reproof, for correction, for instruction in righteousness." The Bible provides us with everything we need to know about God. He wants us to rely on it. Psalm 119:105 says, "Thy word is a lamp unto my feet, and a light unto my path." How blessed are we that we get a lantern for God to guide our way. Take advantage of that, and let God light your path.

King Solomon, most known for his wisdom, instructs us to value the words of our Father and to keep them always close. "My son, attend to my words; incline thine ear unto my sayings. Let them not depart from thine eyes; keep them in the midst of thine heart. For they are life unto those that find them, and health to all their flesh" (Proverbs 4:20–22). Our very health relies on knowing God's Word.

Psalm 119:11 tells us that keeping God's Word in our hearts helps us not to sin—that's a pretty good reason to memorize

Scripture: "Thy word have I hid in mine heart, that I might not sin against thee."

Learning and memorizing Scripture is the best way to keep His Word hidden in our hearts—that way we have access to it at all times. My time in the military provided a lot of experience with memorization. We were all required to remember our personal service number, and we also had to memorize the serial numbers of certain weapons. To ensure that we memorized these things, we were constantly asked to recite this information until we could prove we remembered it fully. Further, we had to memorize drill orders, and we were driven continually to apply these orders promptly and perfectly. And we were also constantly bombarded with information about weapons and their functions, proper techniques to apply on the battlefield, and scores of other critical data to understand and memorize daily. Knowing this information was crucial to survival, just like knowing the Bible is vital to our spiritual survival.

I have been reading the Bible since I came to know Jesus forty-four years ago. I've read the entire Bible several times—I've lost count how many. A wise man told me not to start at Genesis, but to start at the Gospel of John, which clearly describes Jesus as the divine Son of God. I've memorized countless verses and passages, which helps keep my heart and mind focused on Him and helps me resist Satan.

When I read the Bible and learn Scripture, I often change it to first person to help me apply the Scripture directly to myself. This is the case with two passages the Holy Ghost told me to read in Ephesians. I felt the Lord urging me to read the passages every night for a year to help me accomplish His will effectively in all that I do and strengthen my resolve to hold fast to all He has promised to me through Jesus Christ. I know, too, that the Holy Ghost encouraged me to memorize these prayers to help equip me for ministry by gaining greater wisdom and understanding of Christ's love when prophesying, praying for others, preaching God's Word, and sharing the gospel of Jesus to unbelievers. I can now recite them from memory, and I now use these Scriptures almost nightly in prayer.

I have added the first-person pronouns in parentheses. I encourage you to try the same when reading and memorizing Scripture.

> Cease not to give thanks for you (me), making mention of you (me) in my prayers;
>
> That the God of our Lord Jesus Christ, the Father of glory, may give unto you (me) the spirit of wisdom and revelation in the knowledge of him:
>
> The eyes of your (my) understanding being enlightened; that ye (I) may know what is the hope of his calling, and what the riches of the glory of his inheritance in the saints,
>
> And what is the exceeding greatness of his power to us-ward (me-ward) who believe, according to the working of his mighty power,
>
> Which he wrought in Christ, when he raised him from the dead, and set him at his own right hand in the heavenly places,
>
> Far above all principality, and power, and might, and dominion, and every name that is named, not only in this world, but also in that which is to come:
>
> And hath put all things under his feet, and gave him to be the head over all things to the church,
>
> Which is his body, the fulness of him that filleth all in all. (Ephesians 1:16–23)

> For this cause I bow my knees unto the Father of our Lord Jesus Christ,
>
> Of whom the whole family in heaven and earth is named,
>
> That he would grant you (me), according to the riches of his glory, to be strengthened with might by his Spirit in the inner man;
>
> That Christ may dwell in your (my) hearts by faith; that ye (I), being rooted and grounded in love,

> May be able to comprehend with all saints what is the breadth, and length, and depth, and height;
>
> And to know the love of Christ, which passeth knowledge, that ye (I) might be filled with all the fulness of God.
>
> Now unto him that is able to do exceeding abundantly above all that we (I) ask or think, according to the power that worketh in us (me),
>
> Unto him be glory in the church by Christ Jesus throughout all ages, world without end. Amen. (Ephesians 3:14–21)

God wants us to meditate on His Word, and He promises it will make us prosperous. Mind you, our idea of prosperous and God's idea may be different, but know that He has your best interests at heart. "This book of the law shall not depart out of thy mouth; but thou shalt meditate therein day and night, that thou mayest observe to do according to all that is written therein: for then thou shalt make thy way prosperous, and then thou shalt have good success" (Joshua 1:8).

Knowing the Bible also provides us with the tools to encourage others, lead others to Christ, and gently correct those who are on the wrong track. Titus 1:9 says Christians must hold fast to the faithful Word, just as soldiers do in combat and other military endeavors. Hold fast and remember how you were trained so you can help others in the military.

Prayer

In war and scary situations, some people find themselves crying out to God for help or safety even though they're not believers. That was not the case with me. I was as lost as a goose in a snowstorm and never uttered a word to God during my time in Vietnam.

I'm sure you've heard that there is power in prayer. Why is there power in prayer? Prayer allows us to talk directly with God. I can't think of a greater privilege.

Jesus Himself gave us a guideline for how to pray in what we now refer to as the Lord's Prayer:

> Our Father who is in heaven,
> hallowed be Your name.
> Your kingdom come;
> Your will be done
> on earth, as it is in heaven.
> Give us this day our daily bread.
> And forgive us our debts,
> As we forgive our debtors.
> And lead us not into temptation,
> But deliver us from evil.
> For Yours is the kingdom and the power and the glory forever. Amen.
> (Matthew 6:9–13, MEV)

He wants us to praise Him, acknowledge His holiness, ask for His will to be done, come to Him for our needs, ask for forgiveness, and ask for protection and strength.

The Bible also gives us other guidelines for prayer, such as humbling ourselves (2 Chronicles 7:14), praying for those who persecute us (Matthew 5:44), persevering in prayer (Luke 18:1), and praying with thanksgiving (Philippians 4:6).

Father God cares about everything in our lives—even the small things—and He wants us to come to Him and ask Him for things in prayer. As indicated in the Lord's Prayer, we are to ask Him to "give us this day our daily bread." I come to the Lord often for my needs.

I came to Him for a home, and He answered in a big way. Nine years ago, Sheila and I wanted to purchase our first house, but we had a limited budget. We prayed and sought the Lord, and He brought it through. Our real estate agent was not shy about telling us that we wouldn't be able to get what we wanted with the budget we had. But we continued to trust in the Lord. Father God brought us to the perfect house, and we were able to purchase it—44 percent off the appraised price. What a miracle and answer to prayer! Then when it came to the loan, we needed a certain interest rate in order to stay within our monthly budget. A loan officer who had been referred to us was unable to give us what we needed, but we remained determined. He was a fellow Christian and told us to keep him in the loop with our progress. The Lord did indeed allow us to get the loan we needed and stay within the confines of our monthly budget. We called the original loan officer to let him know, and his faith was encouraged by what the Lord had done for us.

Have faith when you pray. If you're going to pray without believing, why even pray? "For verily I say unto you, That whosoever shall say unto this mountain, Be thou removed, and be thou cast into the sea; and shall not doubt in his heart, but shall believe that those things which he saith shall come to pass; he shall have whatsoever he saith. Therefore I say unto you, What things soever ye desire, when ye pray, believe that ye receive them, and ye shall have them" (Mark 11:23–24).

Prayer is one of the essential things Christians must have in their lives, and it is a weapon. Through prayer, we draw closer to Him. I'm sure you've noticed that the way to grow closer to your loved ones is to talk to them. The more we talk to our loved ones, the more our relationship grows. The same is true with God.

Jesus prayed to His Father in the garden of Gethsemane before His crucifixion. He gained strength from His Father by praying "nevertheless not as I will, but as thou wilt" (Matthew 26:39). I say confidently that Jesus gained strength from this prayer because He urged His disciples in Matthew 26:41 to "watch and pray" because "the Spirit is indeed willing but the flesh is weak." So, since we know that Jesus, during His time on Earth, had to battle with human weakness (Matthew 26:39, Hebrews 4:15), we know that He needed to watch and pray to gain strength against His weak flesh in the same way as He urged His disciples to do. Thus, if our perfect, sinless Lord strengthened Himself through prayer, so should we. None of us has to bear the burden our Savior did, yet we all need strength to live out His will, to endure trials, and to resist temptation.

The Bible tells us that Jesus would withdraw by Himself to go pray in the wilderness (Luke 5:16). Friends, follow the model of Jesus. Find consistent time to be alone with God. Each morning when I wake up, I ask God how He wants me to spend time alone with Him. And I pray each evening as I end my day.

And though we should set aside a specific time and place for prayer, that is not the only time to pray. The Bible tells us to pray "always" (Ephesians 6:18) and to "pray without ceasing" (1 Thessalonians 5:17). Have conversation with God throughout your day. I have an attitude of prayer throughout my day, communicating with God in my mind and my heart.

I also have a set time each Friday evening to pray with my wife and son. Before we pray, I play worship music to set the atmosphere. Then we pray whatever Holy Ghost prompts us to pray. Sometimes people text us their prayers so that we can intercede for them. Jesus blesses us when we gather together for prayer. In Matthew 18:20, He says, "For where two or three are gathered together in my name, there am I in the midst of them."

By prayer, we as believers are able to remain in Him and bear spiritual fruit. "I am the vine, ye are the branches: He that abideth in me, and I in him, the same bringeth forth much fruit: for without me ye can do nothing" (John 15:5). Grapes can't grow if the branches aren't connected to the vine. Likewise, we can't bear fruit as Christians if we aren't connected to Him. Our fruit shows others that we love God. The fruit of the Spirit is love, joy, peace, long suffering (patience), gentleness, goodness, faith, meekness, temperance (Galatians 5:22–23). I want to be identified with these characteristics, as I'm sure you do too, and we cannot do it on our own. This can only come through the Holy Spirit and through prayer.

When I pray, I sometimes pray in tongues, as Holy Ghost gifted me with the ability to speak in tongues. Years ago I met a woman who spoke in tongues, and she asked me if I also wanted the gift.

My church denomination at that time didn't believe in the gift of tongues, but I've learned that it is a gift all believers can have. First Corinthians 14 provides an overview of tongues from Paul. Tongues is a beautiful spiritual language between the believer and God for personal edification of the believer. There are times that Holy Ghost gives the interpretation of tongues, but usually only God understands: "For he that speaketh in an unknown tongue speaketh not unto men, but unto God: for no man understandeth him; howbeit in the spirit he speaketh mysteries" (1 Corinthians 14:2). When I pray in tongues, I feel amazingly uplifted and filled with strength. If you want the gift of tongues, ask and you shall receive.

A buddy from New Orleans and I befriended a young Vietnamese boy

At Blackhorse base camp with Doc and another buddy

A buddy and I with 45 pistols at Blackhorse base camp

Dressed in my fatigues in Vietnam

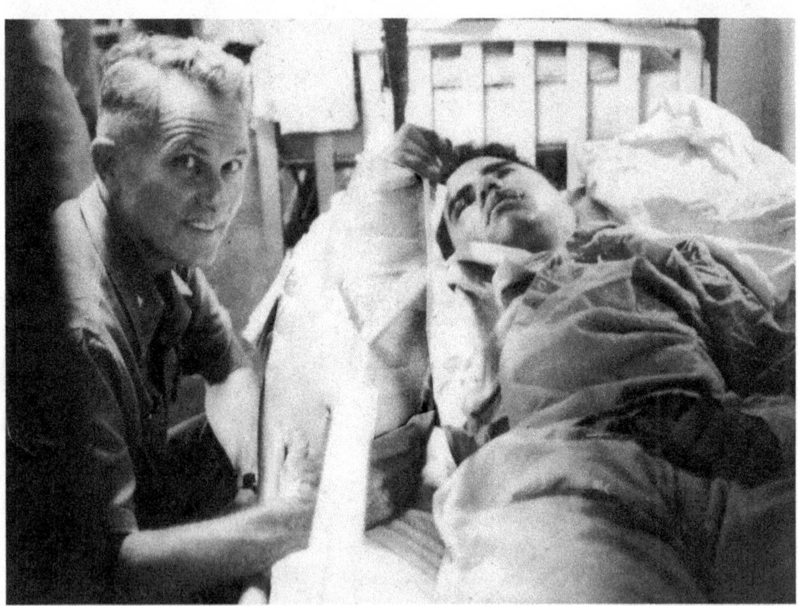

Receiving Purple Heart from Marine Corps Colonel just after being wounded - U.S.S. Repose hospital ship, 1968

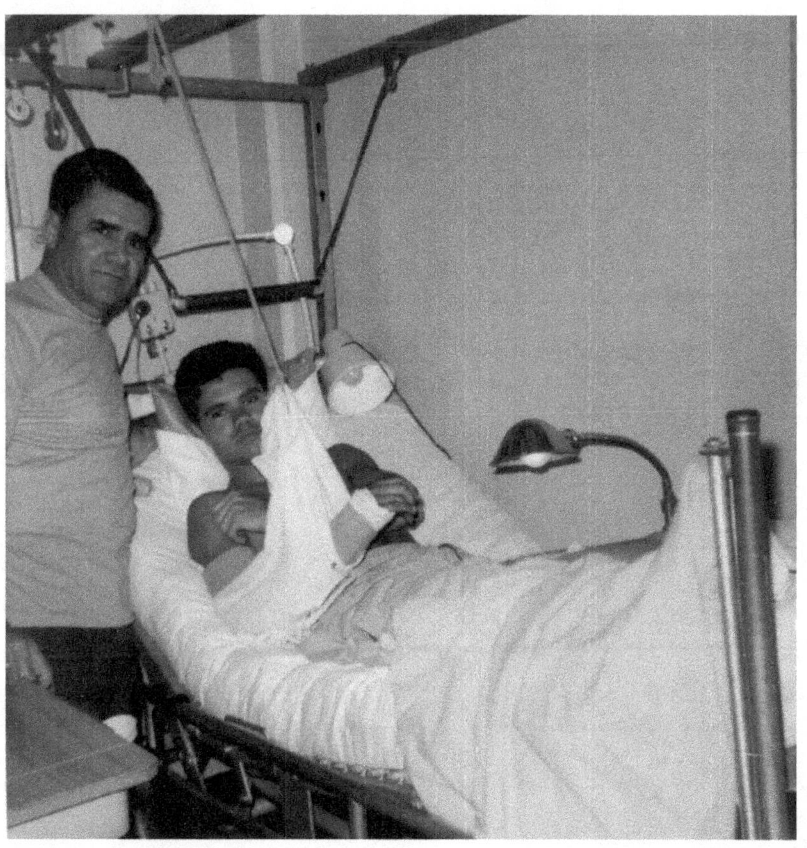

My father, Hampton Boudreaux, Jr., visiting me just after receiving Skin Graft for war wounds - Brooke General Hospital, San Antonio, TX, 1968

Now ambulatory after surgeries from war wounds - Brooke General Hospital, San Antonio, TX, 1968

★ ★ CHAPTER 6
WARFARE INTERCESSION

Wherefore he is able also to save them to the uttermost that come unto God by him, seeing he ever liveth to make intercession for them.
Hebrews 7:25

WHEN IN VIETNAM, WE ENCOUNTERED mortar fire after we landed the boats. We off-loaded our tracks and tanks on a sandy place, Qua Viet. Suddenly, mortar fire came down. The order came over the horn (radio) to keep moving. And we did just that. If one mortar round hit a track or tank, it was over, and we had all our ammunition on the floor of that track. It was very dangerous. The enemy had a forward observer (FO) to spot for artillery to drop on our positions. The FO would call in the position of the enemy, which was us.

Likewise, we drop mortars against the Enemy of our souls—the devil—and a lot of times we drop bigger artillery than mortars. It is called intercession. As Christians, we have so many weapons at our disposal.

Prayer Warriors

Google Dictionary defines *intercede* as to "intervene on behalf of others." Intercessory prayer allows us to pray and plead with God for our needs or for the needs of others. And through warfare intercessory prayer, we pray to conquer evil forces and against spiritual wickedness. Some people use the term *supplication* to pray for ourselves, but I use the term *intercession* to refer to prayer for myself and for others.

I am a prayer warrior, always cognizant of the constant battle of good and evil, and I continuously engage in intercessory prayer. Sometimes we must contend for our faith or the faith of others through prayer. It brings encouragement. When we contend, we fight, fight! Amazing things happen when we intercede.

We have the best advocate interceding for us. Jesus prayed for people while He was on earth, and now that He lives in heaven, He prays for us there. Romans 8:34 says Jesus sits at the right hand of the Father to intercede for us: "Who is he that condemneth? It is Christ that died, yea rather, that is risen again, who is even at the right hand of God, who also maketh intercession for us." And when we don't even know what to pray for ourselves, the Holy Spirit does. "Likewise the Spirit also helpeth our infirmities: for we know not what we should pray for as we ought: but the Spirit itself maketh intercession for us with groanings which cannot be uttered. And he that searcheth the hearts knoweth what is the mind of the Spirit, because he maketh intercession for the saints according to the will of God" (Romans 8:26–27). Notice the word *saints*. Paul said in Romans 1:7 that we are saints. We do not have to die as martyrs or do miracles to be saints. However, we do have to separate ourselves from the world (James 1:27).

Intercessors, we are called prayer warriors. We go to battle with no carnal weapons. In the name of Jesus, we pray for ourselves and for others. The Spirit of God lives in us because we are born-again believers in Jesus, and Christ intercedes for us. We listen to Holy Spirit, and we will know when it is time for combat. But we need to know that we are one with Him.

The story of Abraham and his nephew, Lot, in Genesis 18, is a powerful Old Testament example of intercessory prayer. Abraham prayed for protection for righteous Lot and his family, as God was going to destroy the town of Sodom for its wicked and sinful ways.

The Lord, indeed, heard Abraham's prayer for Lot and his family. There were three spiritual beings that appeared to Abraham. One was the Son of God, even in that day. We call this type of encounter a Christophany—that is, an appearance of Christ. The other two were angels who appeared later to Lot and his family and told them to leave Sodom. Then, destruction came suddenly on those cities. Though the Lord got Lot's family out of there, we see in Genesis 18:32 that God destroyed Sodom and Gomorrah anyway. He is a just God.

The apostle Paul instructs his spiritual son, Timothy, to intercede for others. First Timothy 2:1 says, "I exhort therefore, that first of all, supplications, prayers, intercessions, and giving of thanks, be made for all men." Paul asked his brothers and sisters in Christ to pray for him so that he would be able to tell others of the good news in Jesus (Ephesians 6:19). Paul also prayed regularly for fellow believers. He prayed for them to gain knowledge, wisdom, and spiritual understanding (Colossians 1:9), that they would be filled with joy and peace and hope (Romans 15:13), that they would experience strength of the Holy Spirit (Ephesians 3:16), and that their love would grow (Philippians 1:9).

One time in Vietnam as I was carrying the M-79 grenade launcher, it accidentally went off, but thankfully it did not explode. It sounded like a thump. When we pray, it will be a spiritual thump on the devil's head. When Jesus sent His disciples to minister in the towns of Israel, they hit Satan with a big thump, as we hear Jesus say in Luke 10:18: "And he said unto them, I beheld Satan as lightning fall from heaven."

Aerial Intercession: Angels

About two o'clock one morning in Vietnam, my platoon sergeant told me to get back to my tank, so I followed orders. Then, I was talking with two new recruits who had just arrived at our troop, and, suddenly, I saw tracers in the sky. I also knew that another troop was in the direction that the tracers were headed. I then told the new guys that a troop was getting hit and said, prophetically, that in another fifteen minutes, we would get hit as well. And it happened to the minute. I have no idea how I knew that, but it had to be from God, even though I didn't yet know Him.

The first mortar round came in the perimeter, and I said, "Someone get on the 50 (50-calibre machine gun)!" But the two guys assigned to the 50 dove into the loader's hatch, and all I saw were four legs sticking up. So I had to get on the 50. I said to myself, "Nobody is getting on this tank!" That night, I fired 1,000 50-calibre machine gun rounds and seventeen 90-millimeter cannon rounds. Nobody got on that tank! The troop commander, my captain, said that I shot too much. But I thought, "Nobody got on that tank."

I had help though. We called in gunships, powerfully armored helicopters. What a sight to see! When the mini gun on a gunship fired, it was like a descending ladder from the chopper. The pilot would fire four ball rounds along with a tracer round, which was used to help him see where the ball rounds were headed. It was all belt ammunition, four ball rounds and one tracer round.

In natural war, the gunship helicopters provided aerial attacks crucial to help us fight. In the same way, believers get help from above. Psalm 121:1–2 says, "I will lift up mine eyes unto the hills, from whence cometh my help. My help cometh from the Lord, which made heaven and earth."

One way the Lord provides help for us is through angels. Many times, my life has been in peril, but God watches, His angels watch. I liken angels to helicopter gunships, and I know a lot about the effectiveness of both helicopters and angels in aerial attacks.

About five years ago, I was in a spiritual battle with perverted, demonic spirits three nights in a row. I'd break out the Word of God and speak, pray, and intercede for myself, but I was losing a lot of sleep and not winning the battle against these forces. On the third night, I went to bed and suddenly another spirit came into my bedroom. But I knew that it was a different spirit; I did not see him, but I felt him. With my head on the pillow, I closed and opened my eyes, still didn't see anything, but I said, "Who are you?"

He said, "I am Michael the Archangel."

I said, "Why are you here? I am insignificant."

He replied, "I came to help you fight." Right then and there, my battle with those demonic spirits ended. God doesn't think any of us are insignificant, and we are all worthy of His help.

For believers, angels do our bidding at times. They help us and protect us. They provide aerial attacks on the devil from God. Psalm 91:11 says, "For he shall give his angels charge over thee, to keep thee in all thy ways."

Though we may not always see angels, they are there and were created by God Himself. Colossians 1:16 says, "For by him were all things created, that are in heaven, and that are in earth, visible and invisible, whether they be thrones, or dominions, or principalities, or powers: all things were created by him, and for him."

Angels appeared throughout the Old Testament and the New Testament, helping people and delivering messages. Just to name a few instances: An angel protected Daniel in the lion's den (Daniel 6:22); God sent an angel to guard the Israelites (Exodus 23:20); an angel provided sustenance to Elijah for his journey (1 Kings 19); an angel delivered the news to Zechariah of the impending birth of his son, who would be known as John the Baptist (Luke 1); the angel Gabriel delivered the news to Mary that she would give birth to Jesus (Luke 1); an angel carried the message of Jesus's birth to the shepherds (Luke 2); and an angel appeared at the tomb to deliver the message of Jesus's resurrection (Matthew 28).[9]

The Bible also tells us that we may have encounters with angels without knowing it. "Be not forgetful to entertain strangers: for thereby some have entertained angels unawares" (Hebrews 13:2).

One of the most powerful mentions of angels is in Jesus's last days. Angels appeared to Jesus on the Mount of Olives "strengthening Him" before His crucifixion and helping Him resist temptation (Luke 22:43).

In the battle I mentioned in Vietnam, I had the attitude that nobody was going to get on my tank. It is the same attitude we must have about the devil; we cannot allow him to come and start to mess with our souls, or he will gain access to our spirits. Not happening with me! So we must fight. It's comforting that we have angels to help us fight.

The Lord told me that Michael will be with me the rest of my life to provide extra help against the devil. Only two angels are named in the Bible: Michael and Gabriel. It's comforting to know that God sent Michael to help me fight the good fight and that He sends angels to help all of us fight.

★ ★ CHAPTER 7

CHALLENGES AND DIFFICULTIES

But the God of all grace, who hath called us unto his eternal glory by Christ Jesus, after that ye have suffered a while, make you perfect, stablish, strengthen, settle you.
1 Peter 5:10

WAR ZONES AREN'T COMFORTABLE, EASY places to reside. Soldiers are called to hardship, and as soldiers of Christ Jesus, we will have a lot of difficulty—or junk, as I call it. The apostle Paul, in writing to his spiritual son, Timothy, says in 2 Timothy 2:3, "Thou therefore endure hardness, as a good soldier of Jesus Christ."

But as I've stated before, we are to keep on fighting. Paul writes in 2 Timothy 4:7, "I have fought a good fight, I have finished my course, I have kept the faith."

Now being militant in the Lord Jesus, I know that Christians must endure hardship at times. And we must endure difficulties to become God's warriors. Although we live in the United States of America and live large lives, hard times do come. Accidents, sickness, and death eventually come to us all.

Of course I endured and saw lots of hardship in Vietnam.

One day in Vietnam, we were on a road in the jungle when the track in front of us was attacked by hornets. The hornets in Vietnam were vicious, and they remind me of the terror caused by hornets in the Bible: "And I will send hornets before thee, which shall drive out the Hivite, the Canaanite, and the Hittite, from before thee" (Exodus 23:28). The track commander received the brunt of the attack. The hornets completely covered him. We beat the hornets with our flak jackets, to no avail. Once they left, we returned to base camp, where a chopper came and took the track commander to the hospital. By his own admission, he nearly died. We fought more than just the Vietcong and the NVA. The jungle is quite a rough experience.

I recollect the difficulty of spending 120 days in the field and bathing only once . . . in a running stream with leeches. Our fatigues were so dirty and saturated with sweat they felt like they could stand up by themselves. Our boots were worn out too. Those were hard times in Vietnam, but nothing compared to other things I experienced.

I also contracted malaria. I was playing football at Black Horse, the base camp for the Eleventh Armored Calvary Regiment, and suddenly I felt like I was burning up. It turned out I had malaria, and I spent two weeks in the hospital with ice packs to lower my fever. Unable to eat, I was fed intravenous fluids. But still there were much worse things than malaria.

After the Tet ambush on us, a soldier I knew was killed. He was a jovial Puerto Rican fellow from New York. He was such a nice guy—full of life, dancing, and cutting up all the time. He had come to Vietnam after I did. I was told to identify his body, but I couldn't bring myself to do it. I wasn't sure what came over me that I couldn't follow my staff sergeant's orders, but I think it must have hit me how permanent death is. I was seeing death all around me.

I sometimes relive some of my toughest wartime experiences. One night we killed nine Charlies, and they killed four of us. We dug a hole with the vehicle track recovery (VTR) to bury the Charlie bodies, and we placed the bodies of our troops in body bags. The death of a person is not a good thing, but thankfully I know now that eternal life is possible. Witnessing and dealing with the death of another can be difficult, but now I have the hope of eternal life that I didn't have in my military days.

I saw and still remember terrible injuries. One of our buck sergeants was sitting on the cargo hatch fully exposed during a firefight and did not listen to what we said about getting down from the hatch. He was shot in the neck and paralyzed. My second lieutenant, a laid-back fellow from California, was killed when seven RPG rockets hit his track. Command tracks had many antennas, and Charlie knew this. The Vietcong were very smart. Taking out a command track and all that is on it not only destroys command operations and communications, it also kills important officers. Unfortunately, my best friend was also on that track and was killed.

Patrick was my best friend in Vietnam. He came to me three times to go to church with him. Three is the number of excellence (Companion Bible, appendix 10, p. 14). Each time, I told him, "No." On the third time, he said something that astounded me, which is hard to do.

He said, "I am going to die in Vietnam."

"Man, you are not going to die. If you die, I will die with you," I exclaimed.

But the truth was, he knew that he would be killed there, while I somehow knew that I would not die in Vietnam. To this day, I have no understanding of how I knew I wouldn't die in Vietnam, but I knew.

We were in a fight against the NVA about ten miles outside of Dong Ha. Patrick was on a command track and armored personnel carrier (APC). Though tracks were armored, the tanks could take much more than tracks. Tracks were built primarily for transporting personnel and made of aluminum. Seven rocket-propelled grenades (RPGs) hit the command track my best buddy was on, and he was killed. I had to drag Patrick's body away from the track, which was on fire and about to blow up. My emotions got the best of me, and I wept for a half hour.

I now believe that Patrick was a born-again believer in Christ Jesus and that I will see him again. His body was dead, but his spirit was present with the Lord in an instant. Hebrews 12:1 states, "Wherefore seeing we are compassed about with so great a cloud of witnesses, let us lay aside every weight, and the sin which doth so easily beset us, and let us run with patience the race that is set before us." We are also told, "Precious in the sight of the Lord is the death of his saints" (Psalm 116:15).

God's Word is filled with what happens with His followers upon death. Second Corinthians 5:6–8 declares, "Therefore we are always confident, knowing that, whilst we are at home in the body, we are absent from the Lord: (For we walk by faith, not by sight:) We are confident, I say, and willing rather to be absent from the body, and to be present with the Lord." I believe there were many who died in Vietnam who believed in the Lord Jesus. No waiting and praying, but they were instantly with our Lord. I will see all my believing comrades again, including Patrick.

I had twenty days left in the country until I was to go home. On the same day I lost my best friend, the call came up for us to mount up. Remember we were in a troop, not a company. I was in the cavalry, the motorized armor unit. We were to attack a village and got in a fight against the NVA about ten miles outside of Dong Ha. The NVA were all over the place, and I lost the will to keep fighting.

The gunner on my right side said, "Why don't you shoot?"

I said, "Why? Everybody else is shooting." I was not a coward, but I gave up the will to fight after just losing my best friend. I was holding my 50-calibre machine gun but not firing it. Consequently, I was suddenly wounded during that battle because I had lost the will to fight. I learned something from that experience: never, never give up the fight. Again, the apostle Paul said, "I have fought a good fight" (Second Timothy 4:7). After I received the Lord Jesus into my life, I settled it in my heart that I would never give up the fight in Christ.

When I was injured, I was thrown back against the cargo hatch and had to kick my track commander to get him to drive back to the medics' track. I took five shots in my right forearm and a bullet in my face. I went to a mobile army surgical hospital, otherwise known as a MASH unit, and realized the extent of my injuries. They put me on the USS *Repose*, a hospital ship anchored in Da Nang Harbor, and a Marine Corps colonel gave me a Purple Heart since I was injured by the enemy. They put me to sleep and cut the bullet out of my face, and they bandaged my arm.

I was transported back on a stretcher to the United States in an AC-141 jet. We flew to Japan and stayed for the night in a hospital there. Then we flew to Oakland, California, and stayed in a hospital. Then we went to San Antonio, Texas, and Brooke General Hospital, and this was where the fun began. I spent five months recovering.

The doctor who worked on me at Brooke General was a colonel. First, he started to dig in my right arm to remove the debris while I was awake. Hello! He had to see which nerves were still alive. Next I had surgery where they removed two strips of skin from my left thigh. One was 7.0 x 1.75 inches, the other 5.0 x 2.25 inches. For three days, the pain was intense on the left leg. I took morphine for pain and used a heat lamp on that leg. At the same time, they were putting the skin on my right arm to cover the holes. Praise the Lord for good doctors. I would do it all again for my nation.

But as painful as that was, it was small stuff compared to some men who lost their feet or arms—or lives. I weep as I write this, and it happened fifty-one years ago. Oh, Beloved, thank those who have served and are serving. I love my country. Praise the Lord for doctors and nurses all over this country who helped the armed forces in every branch.

Father God spared my life. Jeremiah 1:5 says, "Before I formed thee in the belly I knew thee; and before thou camest forth out of the womb I sanctified thee, and I ordained thee a prophet unto the nations." Long before I knew anything about what God would do with me, He had it in His mind already—before He formed me in my mother's belly. That is our God. What a God we serve!

The hedge of protection that the Lord has over and around us is powerful, but He will take it away at times, to teach us to obey Him.

In the book of Job, Satan got permission from the Lord to attack Job. Satan believed that Job was upright, blameless, and righteous because God had blessed him with wealth, success, and an easy life. He thought if God removed the hedge of protection around him, Job would curse God. In Job 1:10, the devil went to God and said, "Has not thou made an hedge about him, and about his house and about all that he hath on every side?" Though the devil took away Job's health, wealth, and family, Job never cursed the Lord.

I had a hedge of protection disappear before my very eyes while in Vietnam. The lieutenant over our platoon knew I was a short-timer. A few days before I was to leave Vietnam, he ordered me to step off the battlefield, board a Chinook helicopter, assist in taking prisoners recently captured back to headquarters, and remain at headquarters out of harm's way. I recall one guy on the helicopter, who was gutshot, tried to get out of the chopper while in the air. But a Marine put a pistol to his head and told him, "Don't you move!" The guy instantly sat back down.

When we landed at headquarters, they took the prisoners off the Chinook. But the sergeant major came up to me and said, "What are you doing here?"

I replied, "I came with the Vietcong."

He said, "Get your butt back out there!" There went my hedge of protection.

For some reason my lieutenant wanted me safe. My lieutenant was trying to protect me because I was short and leaving Vietnam soon. But the sergeant major knew nothing about me and how many days I had left. Though I was wounded with just twenty days left in Vietnam, my heavenly Father protected me, and I never saw death. (Also of note is that the lieutenant I was referred to was killed the same day I was wounded along with my best friend, Patrick; they were on the same track.)

Even though I didn't know the Lord Jesus, God the Father had a plan for me. The plan was that I get wounded and live to talk about it. When a person goes through something as traumatic as war and is wounded, or other experiences as traumatic as those things are, God has something to say through that individual.

Father God will allow difficulties and hardships to those who are coming into His kingdom and to those who are already in His kingdom. He knows those who are His and will both allow and cause negative experiences to occur in the lives of His sons and daughters. Hebrews 12:6 says, "For whom the Lord loveth he chasteneth and scourges every son whom he receiveth." We have a heavenly Father unlike our earthly fathers. Our heavenly Father has a far greater purpose. Hebrews 12:10 states, "For they verily for a few days chastened us after their own pleasure; but he for our profit, that we might be partakers of his holiness." Further, Hebrews 12:8 says we should want chastisement. Oh, that we be treated as sons and not illegitimate. Also, verse 11 of Hebrews 12 says if we allow chastening, which seems painful rather than pleasant, it will yield the peaceable fruit of righteousness for us as God's children.

The Bible has several Scriptures instructing us to rejoice in our sufferings. Though suffering isn't fun or what we would choose, it can increase our faith if we let it. James 1:2–3 says, "My brethren, count it all joy when ye fall into divers temptations; Knowing this, that the trying of your faith worketh patience." Likewise, Romans 5:3–5 says, "And not only so, but we glory in tribulations also: knowing that tribulation worketh patience; And patience, experience; and experience, hope: And hope maketh not ashamed; because the love of God is shed abroad in our hearts by the Holy Ghost which is given unto us."

When I was wounded in Vietnam but saved from death, I did not know at the time why God saved my life, but I now know He wasn't finished with me.

With rest in Jesus the Christ, we can endure difficulties as soldiers and warriors of Christ. But the rest of God is a powerful thing that we must labor to attain. Paul writes in Hebrews 4:11, "Let us labor therefore to enter into that rest, lest any man fall after the same example of unbelief." It takes faith to enter that rest. First, we must read about it in God's Word, then have faith that Paul was inspired by Holy Ghost to write about God's rest. We endure in the same way as we did as warriors in Vietnam, in World Wars I and II, and in every other conflict we have experienced since this nation was formed.

★ ★ CHAPTER 8

MONSOONS, ANTS, AND TUNNELS

God is our refuge and strength, a very present help in trouble.
Psalm 46:1

MONSOONS IN VIETNAM—WHAT A TRIP they were. We experienced six months of rain daily; then the dry season followed. It was not easy walking in mud up to your calves. Yet this was war, and in war there is much trouble, from the enemy and from nature. In that part of the world, these monsoons occur all the time. However, in the United States, this type of weather does not happen as severely. When it does, many daily operations cease. When it rains in Vietnam, it is not April showers; it is pelting rain for long periods. In fact, one time, because of the torrential rain, I got out of my track with a bar of soap, showered, and enjoyed the opportunity to get extra clean.

The Bible talks about storms. God told Noah to build an ark of gopher wood because He was sending a storm that would flood the world: "Make thee an ark of gopher wood; rooms shalt thou make in the ark, and shalt pitch it within and without with pitch" (Genesis 6:14). It was precise. God is that way. When God sent the rain in that day, it was indeed a monsoon. Forty days and nights of rain brought a flood, killing the wicked from the earth.

Much rain in Vietnam, much rain in Noah's day, and my Father starts it all to destroy the Enemy of our souls and to help grow crops.

In Job 37:5–14, we see clearly that the Lord controls the weather for purposes of correction, love, and the land. My God is an awesome God! All Father God wants is righteousness. Noah was a preacher of righteousness (2 Peter 2:5). From Adam and Eve to this day, all Father God wants is righteousness.

I have never before and still have never experienced the kind of rain I encountered in Vietnam; however, that rain is not to be compared to the rain that came down in Noah's day, which killed all of mankind. All inhabitants of the earth today need to realize that it is God's earth and that He wants righteousness. After all, the earth is part of His kingdom.

If God the Father can destroy mankind and His creation, as He did with the flood in Genesis, then I believe He can save all of mankind. That is why Jesus came to earth 2,000 years ago. Genesis 6:7 states, "And the Lord said, I will destroy man whom I have created from the face of the earth; both man, and beast, and the creeping thing, and the fowls of the air; for it repenteth me that I have made them."

Biblical storms in the New Testament represent life's troubles and fears. When the storms of life and war pelt us, our houses can survive and thrive if our foundation is on God.

> And the rain descended, and the floods came, and the winds blew, and beat upon that house; and it fell not: for it was founded upon a rock. And every one that heareth these sayings of mine, and doeth them not, shall be likened unto a foolish man, which built his house upon the sand: And the rain descended, and the floods came, and the winds blew, and beat upon that house; and it fell: and great was the fall of it. (Matthew 7:25–27)

If our faith remains in God, heavy rains and storms will not cause our house to fall. A sturdy foundation—reading His Word, obeying Him, praying in the Spirit—will keep our faith strong throughout life's heavy rains and storms. Will you and your house stand firm, or will you fear when storms arise?

Fear

Our natural tendency is to fear when things seem out of control. Even Jesus's disciples who walked daily with Him feared at times.

> And when he was entered into a ship, his disciples followed him. And, behold, there arose a great tempest in the sea, insomuch that the ship was covered with the waves: but he was asleep. And his disciples came to him, and awoke him, saying, Lord, save us: we perish. And he saith unto them, Why are ye fearful, O ye of little faith? Then he arose, and rebuked the winds and the sea; and there was a great calm. But the men marvelled, saying, What manner of man is this, that even the winds and the sea obey him! (Matthew 8:23–27)

We all encounter storms in life. Learn from what Jesus told His disciples; He wants us to keep our faith in Him and trust in Him even when things seem out of control and scary.

War is grueling and scary. When I first got to Vietnam, we had an eight-day training period. Several other men and I had to go through this training. We did foot patrols in the jungle and one day in a rubber-tree plantation. It was grueling. They made me carry the M-60 machine gun and two bandoliers of ammunition. Our superiors knew beforehand where we were going to be posted. So we were trained for that position. I needed help carrying that M-60 machine gun, a heavy weapon for jungle warfare.

The Tet Offensive was particularly frightening. When the Tet Offensive happened, I think we were at Black Horse, the Eleventh Armored Cavalry Regiment's base camp in Vietnam. The Tet Offensive was coordinated by the NVA simultaneously on more than 100 South Vietnamese cities so that the United States would begin withdrawing. We would have thunder runs and night patrols in our tracks and tanks in columns. Charlie hid in what we called windrows and ambushed our columns. The windrows were cut-down trees that were stacked in rows. Charlie would hide in these windrows with rocket-propelled grenades (RPGs) and ambush our people.

To pull off something as massive as the Tet Offensive was ingenious, to say the least. All over South Vietnam, the Tet Offensive happened at the same time. President Ho Chi Minh, the ruler of North Vietnam at the time of the war, had it going on! Tet is their Lunar New Year holiday. We paid dearly for that New Year; many fireworks going on. We lost many in those battles, but so did they. It was a turning point in the war. But I like to give credit where it is due.

Once when I was on foot patrol in the jungle with a lieutenant, a snake fell from a tree onto the lieutenant's back. That man tore his shirt off so fast. I never saw anything like it in my life. That man never came on foot patrol with us again. Do not let your fear stop you from doing your duty in God.

Additionally, I remember a tanker or tank commander coming on that same patrol with us. I had never seen this before. But the lieutenant insisted that the tanker come along on this foot patrol. This tank commander shot his M-16 rifle, acting as if we were being attacked to persuade the lieutenant to go back to the unit position to get out of the jungle. I laugh at this even now. The lieutenant was green and wanted to set up an ambush. But the tank commander said it was too big a force to ambush a Vietcong. In other words, "Let's get the heck out of Dodge!" The tank commander's argument was that tankers did not go on foot patrols; they wanted to stay put on the tank. The tankers were short-timers, but the men on tracks, like me, were on foot patrols all the time. Truthfully, I never understood this argument from tank commanders. They felt that they should not go on foot patrols, but we were all in the same cavalry outfit where we were all required to do foot patrols.

Honestly, I believe that at the root of their argument was fear. Fear is common. It can paralyze a person unless he gets a hold of himself. I did not want to set up an ambush for the Vietcong either, as I did not see any of them around.

The apostle Paul said to Timothy, his spiritual son, "For God hath not given us the spirit of fear; but of power, and of love, and of a sound mind" (2 Timothy 1:7). There are many things that bring fear on saints of God in the body of Christ. Many believers fear that they will never become the man or woman that God has called them to be. Others fear they will fall from grace or be called a nut by someone. Fear of man shows itself in many ways; you name it, the fear of man is behind it.

But God has not given us fear. It is a spirit from the devil himself. Fear can paralyze us from doing what God has called us to do. As a called prophet of God, I was afraid to speak for God. So we may make excuses for not speaking the truth. But truth comes from the Lord Jesus Himself alone. If you see the Enemy or a spirit working in someone, we must speak the truth—not to embarrass anyone, but to truly help that person.

The Truth is a person; He is God's Son, Jesus Christ. On that foot patrol, fear came to me when the lieutenant wanted to set up an ambush for the Vietcong, but I was going to do it in spite of fear. We must learn to fight through fear, whatever it may be. Beloved, for Christians, the sting of death is gone, as it should be. In 1 Corinthians 15:55, it says, "O death, where is thy sting? O grave, where is thy victory?"

Faith and Perseverance

One day, we were "busting jungle." In cavalry outfits, there are tanks and tracks that can be used as bulldozers. We started to knock down a tree that had an ant nest in it. The nest came down, and the ants were ticked off, and I got the brunt of their animosity. I hate ants anyway, but the ants in Vietnam were a whole different breed, and they bit hard. Within seconds, I had all my clothes off, trying to get the ants off.

The Bible talks about ants in Proverbs 6:6–11. Verse 6 states, "Go to the ant, thou sluggard; consider her ways, and be wise." Ants are very industrious, hardworking creatures; they build their homes.

In Vietnam, their homes were in trees, whereas in the United States, their homes are on the ground. Ants build and gather food. I have read that there are soldier ants, and their massive jaws are made for battle and to attack their prey. The ants in Vietnam made war, and they did not know when to quit. We need to be like the ant. We need to make war against the devil and not quit.

That day in Vietnam, the ants made war on me to protect what they had. In the same way, I believe that the United States went to Vietnam to fight to protect our way of life in this beautiful country of ours. Communism is not of God, but God is sovereign; He does and permits all that He pleases. Psalm 24:1 declares, "The earth is the LORD's, and the fulness thereof; the world, and they that dwell therein." Yet, some do not know that the earth belongs to the Lord God, Jesus, His Son, and Holy Ghost. But one day the whole world will know, even the ant. And like the ant, we need to keep fighting against our Enemy.

Paul persevered through many troubles for the kingdom of God. Through much tribulation, we must keep going to see God's kingdom (Acts 14:22). It is an ongoing kingdom. The apostle Paul knew that he was putting kingdom people in prison and holding the coats for people to stone them to death—kingdom people like Stephen. But as a former pastor of ours said many times, "God knocked Paul off his horse and sent his saddle home." But the point in the saying was not about a literal horse or saddle; it was about the Lord Jesus confronting and changing Paul. Acts 9:3–4 says, "And as he (Paul) journeyed, he came near Damascus: and suddenly there shined round about him a light from heaven: And he fell to the earth and heard a voice saying unto him, Saul, Saul, why persecutest thou me?"

It is said that Paul, who was Saul, wrote two-thirds of the New Testament. A man who persecuted the true church of the living God wrote all that for us after he converted to Christianity. He was beaten, shipwrecked, often hungry, and endured all kinds of other troubles. Yet he persevered for the love of God, Jesus and Holy Ghost. Paul and the Lord Jesus are two true examples of perseverance, as are all the prophets, apostles, and saints of God.

But we look to Jesus, the Author and Finisher of our faith. Beloved, have no fear. Perfect love is the love of God. First John 4:18 says, "There is no fear in love; but perfect love casteth out fear: because fear hath torment. He that feareth is not made perfect in love." The Lord's work does not stop at merely reading His Word. I must believe; we must believe. This is faith. Because He continues, we can continue. The Bible says, "The Lord killeth, and maketh alive: he bringeth down to the grave, and bringeth up." (1 Samuel 2:6). Man does not have that ability. Man may declare, "Be raised from the dead", but God is the one who does the miracle. So, by Christ's blood, we are healed and raised from the dead, in the name of Jesus. God's Word revives!

The Holy Scriptures are so unique that it is impossible to please God without faith, according to Hebrews 11:6. Now pay attention to these verses, and you will be blessed. In Galatians 5:6 it reads, "For in Jesus Christ neither circumcision availeth any thing, nor uncircumcision; but faith which worketh by love." How neat is that? You cannot have faith without love, nor can you have love without faith. Like love and marriage, they go together; that is, marriage in God: A man to a woman, not man to man or woman to woman.

Your faith that comes from the Lord Jesus only works by love. The gift of Holy Ghost works by faith, and faith works by love —God's love. Even the gifts of Jesus—apostle, prophet, evangelist, pastor, and teacher—work by faith. Faith works by love. If you don't have love, you don't have faith.

Narrow Is the Way

While in Vietnam, I was told to crawl into tunnels like a tunnel rat looking for weapons. The Vietnamese were a very industrious people. They had hospitals underground for the wounded. In other tunnels, they housed weapons. I remember us capturing 1,000 weapons in one tunnel complex. Now, these tunnels were not big freeway tunnels or other modern concrete enclosures as you may think of today. These were extremely dark, narrow, underground tunnels in the jungle constructed by the enemy for hiding soldiers and weapon caches. Thankfully, I only tunnel-crawled twice—that was enough.

At the time I was five feet, nine inches and weighed about 120 pounds—not a big guy, but it was still narrow and difficult. Rat tunnel duty was miserable and resembled hell to me. In an odd way, my experience reminds me of Jesus's words about narrow paths in Matthew 7. Though His path is narrow, it is also rewarding and life-giving. Jesus tells us that many take the easy, wider path that doesn't lead to Him. The path to Him is smaller and more difficult, yet it leads to eternal life. "Enter ye in at the strait gate: for wide is the gate, and broad is the way, that leadeth to destruction, and many there be which go in thereat: Because strait is the gate, and narrow is the way, which leadeth unto life, and few there be that find it" (Matthew 7:13–14).

★ ★ CHAPTER 9

FOOLS, FOLLY, AND SIN

Repent ye therefore, and be converted, that your sins may be blotted out, when the times of refreshing shall come from the presence of the Lord.
Acts 3:19

WHILE IN VIETNAM, WE HAD the opportunity to go to a different location for a time of rest and recuperation. I went to Hong Kong, China. While in Hong Kong, I started a fight with a Chinese man. It was foolish, and I should never have done it, and I paid a stiff price for it. The Chinese man came after me with two of his friends, followed me, then hit me with a bamboo pole that was four inches in diameter. The pole separated into many splits when it hit me. After they hit me on the head, I bowed down and started to fight with them. Then I saw the bamboo pole that they had used to hit that hard Boudreaux head. But I fought as best I could and caught a rickshaw back to the motel. When I returned to the motel, I slumped onto the hood of a car. Two warrant officers found me and brought me to a British-run hospital. The doctor told me I had a mild concussion. The Lord even watches over fools. Those men could have killed me. Yet in retrospect, God had a plan. And I know I'm forgiven for what I originally did to that man. That's the beauty of Christ—He forgives us even when we don't deserve it. Even with a hard head, Father God watched over me.

Blunders happen all the time in war or in peace. We were on a foot patrol in the jungle one day, and I was carrying the M-79 grenade launcher. After fording a stream, I raised my leg on the stream's bank, and when I placed the weapon on my thigh, it fired because, of course, the safety was off, but I didn't realize it. After it fired, the man in front of me exclaimed, "Boudreaux!" But, praise the Lord Jesus, the grenade did not explode; it simply skittered for about thirty yards and just lay there. For this weapon to work effectively, I would have had to launch it at an angle and about fifty yards from the target, similar to a mortar.

Human beings will all make mistakes; we blunder. And sometimes our blunders are more than just mistakes—sometimes they are outright sin. But Jesus said, "Repent." If we do not repent, we will all likewise perish (Luke 13:3).

The Lord asked me to share yet another story with you about sin, though it is crude. In Vietnam at the Bearcat base camp, located in a town near Saigon called Biên Hòa, the latrines were outhouses, and the feces that went in there had to be burned. I had that duty one time and only one time. I was private first class, and the private had to pull that kind of duty on occasion. To burn the feces, we had to use diesel fuel because it burns long. We would set it on fire, and it would burn all day long. Sin and iniquity are refuse and must be done away with.

The Bible says in Hebrews 12:29, "For our God is a consuming fire." Verse 28 says, "Wherefore we receiving a kingdom which cannot be moved, let us have grace, whereby we may serve God acceptably with reverence and godly fear."

God wants to burn up refuse—sin and wickedness—all things that are not in His kingdom. Galatians 5:19–21 says, "Now the works of the flesh are manifest, which are these; Adultery, fornication, uncleanness, lasciviousness, Idolatry, witchcraft, hatred, variance, emulations, wrath, strife, seditions, heresies, Envyings, murders, drunkenness, revellings, and such like: of the which I tell you before, as I have also told you in time past, that they which do such things shall not inherit the kingdom of God."

God hates sin and wants it gone. But the miracle of God is that He forgives our sin. We see examples of sin throughout the Bible. God's Word makes it clear that He despises lying and deceit, but He's a just God and looks at the heart.

Biblical Sin

Members of the early church pooled their resources and sold their excess to help feed the hungry and poor. Acts 5 tells us that Ananias and Sapphira lied to Peter, and ultimately to the Holy Ghost, saying that they had sold what they had and gave everything when in reality, they had kept back some of the money. Consequently, God killed Ananias first, and then He killed Sapphira. While this may seem harsh, it lets us know that God does not want us lying to Him. Had they been forthcoming about their decision to keep some of the money, I am confident that the outcome would have been different. Beloved, learn from this. Do not be a hypocrite, acting holy while harboring deceit. The punishment will, indeed, be harsh.

But take heart—in spite of our sins, God looks at the heart. The Bible's King David is a perfect example. King David had many foolish moments and blunders—sin—yet he is still known as being a man after God's heart. He was king because God made him king, and God chose him (1 Samuel 16:13). God not only chose him to be king, but He chose him to be in the lineage of Christ (Matthew 1:6) despite all his sin. Of David, the Bible says, "But the LORD said unto Samuel, Look not on his countenance, or on the height of his stature; because I have refused him: for the LORD seeth not as man seeth; for man looketh on the outward appearance, but the LORD looketh on the heart" (1 Samuel 16:7).

David was the apple of God's eye (Psalm 17:8), yet he greatly failed the Lord.

In 2 Samuel 11, we read about David having an adulterous affair with Bathsheba while Uriah the Hittite, her husband, was off to war. Second Samuel 11:1 says, "And it came to pass, after the year was expired, at the time when kings go forth to battle, that David sent Joab, and his servants with him, and all Israel; and they destroyed the children of Ammon, and besieged Rabbah. But David tarried still at Jerusalem."

There lies the problem: David stayed home. The king should have gone to war with his men, but he stayed home. The Bible says in Revelation 1:6, "And [Jesus] hath made us kings and priests unto God and his Father; to him be glory and dominion forever and ever. Amen."

So while David stayed home, he looked across the way and saw Uriah's wife, the beautiful Bathsheba, bathing on the rooftop of her house, and David gave in to his temptation. Bathsheba became pregnant with David's child. Second Samuel 11:5 says, "And the woman conceived, and sent and told David, and said, I am with child." So David began conspiring. King David attempted a coverup by sending for Uriah to be with Bathsheba. But Uriah was such an honorable man that he would not sleep with his wife during wartime. Apparently David knew nothing of this man's sterling character.

Verse 9 says, "But Uriah slept at the door of the king's house with all the servants of his lord, and went not to his house." This story reeks of David's deception. We have a price to pay when we do not walk in the ways of the kingdom of God, which is righteousness, peace, and joy in the Holy Ghost (Romans 14:17).

Uriah the Hittite was such an honorable soldier. Oh, to be a soldier like that! His name means the light of Jehovah. I know we have men and women who have hearts like that who serve in the armed services. But they need to see Jesus the Christ. David wrote a letter to Joab and sent it by Uriah (2 Samuel 11:14–15). In the letter was Uriah's death sentence. Uriah did not look at the letter. What a man of God, full of integrity!

In 2 Samuel 11:27, the Bible says that God was displeased with David. The Lord then sent Nathan the prophet to confront David because of his sin. The prophet then told David a story that

I like to call "Rich Man, Poor Man" because the story is about how a rich man takes advantage of a poor man and his family by taking a lamb from that family to feed a traveler rather than using his own lambs (2 Samuel 12). Then, David condemned himself with his own lips by stating that this rich man should pay for his sins (2 Samuel 12:5–6). Of course, in verse 7 of this chapter, David is then informed that he is the wicked "rich man" in the story because of his sin against this family and the Lord. Next, the Lord spoke through Nathan: "Now therefore the sword shall never depart from thine house; because thou hast despised me, and hast taken the wife of Uriah the Hittite to be thy wife" (2 Samuel 12:10). As further consequence for David's sin, Bathsheba and David's baby was then killed by the Lord (2 Samuel 12:15–18).

After reading about David and his actions, we find that God is God. He will not put up with our sinful ways. Yet despite great sin, God still loves us and will forgive us when we repent.

David received forgiveness from God after admitting and repenting of his sin, as the Lord told him through Nathan the prophet: "And Nathan said unto David, The Lord also hath put away thy sin; thou shalt not die" (2 Samuel 12:13). When we fail the Lord, if we ask forgiveness and repent, God the Father will forgive our sins. "If we confess our sins, he is faithful and just to forgive us our sins, and to cleanse us from all unrighteousness" (1 John 1:9).

Psalm 51 is David's prayer after sinning with Bathsheba—his confession, request for mercy, and appeal for God to purify him.

> Have mercy upon me, O God, according to thy lovingkindness: according unto the multitude of thy tender mercies blot out my transgressions.
>
> Wash me thoroughly from mine iniquity, and cleanse me from my sin.
>
> For I acknowledge my transgressions: and my sin is ever before me.

Against thee, thee only, have I sinned, and done this evil in thy sight: that thou mightest be justified when thou speakest, and be clear when thou judgest.

Behold, I was shapen in iniquity; and in sin did my mother conceive me.

Behold, thou desirest truth in the inward parts: and in the hidden part thou shalt make me to know wisdom.

Purge me with hyssop, and I shall be clean: wash me, and I shall be whiter than snow.

Make me to hear joy and gladness; that the bones which thou hast broken may rejoice.

Hide thy face from my sins, and blot out all mine iniquities.

Create in me a clean heart, O God; and renew a right spirit within me.

Cast me not away from thy presence; and take not thy holy spirit from me.

Restore unto me the joy of thy salvation; and uphold me with thy free spirit.

Then will I teach transgressors thy ways; and sinners shall be converted unto thee.

Deliver me from bloodguiltiness, O God, thou God of my salvation: and my tongue shall sing aloud of thy righteousness.

O Lord, open thou my lips; and my mouth shall shew forth thy praise.

For thou desirest not sacrifice; else would I give it: thou delightest not in burnt offering.

The sacrifices of God are a broken spirit: a broken and a contrite heart, O God, thou wilt not despise.

Do good in thy good pleasure unto Zion: build thou the walls of Jerusalem.

Then shalt thou be pleased with the sacrifices of righteousness, with burnt offering and whole burnt offering: then shall they offer bullocks upon thine altar. (Psalm 51:1–19)

Because Jesus died on the cross for us, we can ask for forgiveness of our sins, like David did, and He wipes the slate clean. "If we confess our sins, he is faithful and just to forgive us our sins, and to cleanse us from all unrighteousness" (1 John 1:9).

Apostles Peter and Judas both sinned against Jesus. The Lord looks at the heart. And He also looks at our reaction to our sin. Peter denied Jesus three times. Jesus told His disciples in Matthew 26:31a, "All ye shall be offended because of me this night." Verse 33 says, "Peter answered and said unto him, Though all men shall be offended because of thee, yet will I never be offended." The Lord knows all men's hearts. In Verse 34, Jesus said to Peter, "Verily I say unto thee, That this night, before the cock crow, thou shalt deny me thrice." If anyone wonders how He knew this, it is through the gift of the word of knowledge. In 1 Corinthians 12:8–10, we see that there are nine gifts of the Holy Ghost, one of which is the "word of knowledge."

Peter did exactly what the Lord said he would do beforehand. He denied that he knew Jesus three times while he watched the Lord Jesus's trial before His crucifixion. We know that he wept at his failure to knowing the Lord (Matthew 26:75) and that he ran to the empty tomb (Luke 24:12), so we know his heart. We also know that Peter went to see Jesus after he appeared to some of the disciples (John 21:7). We are to go to Jesus when we sin, and we are to repent. Jesus then asked Peter three times if he loved him, to which Peter answered yes, and He commissioned him to "feed my sheep" (John 21:17). Peter went on to write two books of the Bible and continued to spread the Word of Jesus.

On the other hand, Judas Iscariot betrayed Jesus by giving Him up for thirty pieces of silver. Jesus told him, "Do what you must do." Like Peter, Judas regretted his actions (Matthew 27:3), but he did not go to Jesus to repent. Instead he took his own life (Matthew 27:5).

Friends, can you understand this? Even being born again and Spirit filled, we will still blow it, but not necessarily to the degree to which Judas or Peter did. People say we must never say never, but I say never all the time. I will never deny Jesus the Christ. We must repent of our sins. Jesus says in Luke 13:3, "I tell you, Nay: but except ye repent, ye shall all likewise perish."

We see countless examples of the folly of humanity before God throughout history, but I am so thankful that Father God loves His people, even when we do costly, foolish things.

Forgiving Others

And while God forgives our sins when we repent, we also must forgive the sins of others. The Bible is filled with verses instructing us to forgive those who have wronged us. For example, Colossians 3:13 says, "Forbearing one another, and forgiving one another, if any man have a quarrel against any: even as Christ forgave you, so also do ye."

And the Bible tells us that if we want to be forgiven, we too must forgive those who sin against us. "And when ye stand praying, forgive, if ye have ought against any: that your Father also which is in heaven may forgive you your trespasses. But if ye do not forgive, neither will your Father which is in heaven forgive your trespasses" (Mark 11:25–26). That's motivation to forgive. There are times where we are wronged and want to get back at the person, but "Vengeance is mine; I will repay, saith the Lord" (Romans 12:19).

Forgiveness is easier for some people than others. For me, it's very difficult, but thankfully, Holy Ghost and I are tight. I don't have it in me to forgive, but I am able to do it through prayer and relying on Him. The Enemy doesn't want us to forgive. He wants us to stay bitter and in bondage instead of experiencing the freedom in forgiveness.

I've had some deep hurts I've had to forgive and learned to press in to Christ to forgive and let go. Deep hurts can take a while to release until we experience the peace of God. Forgiving my dad took a lot of perseverance in prayer. As I've said, he wasn't a good dad, and his family was not a priority for him. Forgiving some of my military officers was also difficult. They didn't always treat us soldiers well. I remember one officer putting out his cigarette on my chest. Though it happened years ago and I would never see him again, God called me to forgive him. I've also had to forgive fellow Christians, such as the pastor who told me I couldn't speak in tongues if I were to stay in that denomination.

All people sin. Forgiveness from our Father is a gift, and we, too, are to pass on that gift, which, ultimately, blesses us.

★ ★ CHAPTER 10

IDENTITY IN CHRIST

But as many as received him, to them gave he power to become the sons of God, even to them that believe on his name.

John 1:12

WE ALL HAVE SEVERAL IDENTITIES and roles. I am a Cajun. My ancestors came from France, so I consider myself French from Rayne, Louisiana. We are called Cajuns, but we are French Americans. I am also a proud husband, a father of six, and a grandfather of ten.

I am also a veteran. One who is in the Marines becomes a Marine. Another in the Navy must become a sailor. If in the Air Force, then one becomes an airman. I enlisted in the army and became a soldier. I still love the US military, and I love our country. I am seventy years old at the time of this writing, and if this nation would recall me to active duty, I would not hesitate to go anywhere. Once a soldier, always a soldier!

When I entered the military, I had to forget that I ever existed as an ordinary person, and I had to reidentify as a soldier. I was no longer a civilian. The reality of laying aside the norms of civilian life is an important aspect of becoming a good soldier. Before enlisting in the army, all I'd known was civilian life; military life is much different. When a civilian becomes a soldier, that person becomes a Government Issue (GI). That person is now, in a sense, the property of the US Government, and that person's life changes forever. That soldier can no longer focus on satisfying personal desires but instead is to work diligently to meet the needs of the country to which that soldier belongs by working together with fellow soldiers and officers.

Soldiers can't even make ordinary choices regarding physical appearance that civilians do. When I became a soldier, I was required to wear a uniform as opposed to everyday clothing, and that uniform must always be worn when the soldier is in service. Additionally, I was given hygienic requirements such as shaving, showering, dressing, etc. These tasks must be daily adhered to with precision. The level of hygienic precision required in military life is much more intense than in most aspects of civilian life. As soon as I joined the army, even my appearance changed.

I was being trained to become what the military expects us to become—killers. In the US Army, regardless of our military occupational specialties (MOSs), we are trained to be killers and that becomes a part of our identity.

And though I am a proud Cajun, husband, father, grandfather, and veteran, I am most proud to be a child of God. Believers in Christ are all children of God.

In Ephesians 2:10, apostle Paul writes, "For we are His workmanship, created in Christ Jesus unto good works, which God hath before ordained that we should walk in them." As His workmanship, we are God's precious creation, and we are to work for Him. Beloved, from day one, we are His workmanship. Our former selves don't matter.

For me, my entrance into the US Army can be compared to my journey to Christianity. I entered the military based on my parents' insistence, and God the Creator insisted that I follow Him. He calls people to serve Him. Don't you just love the way He is? He is the Way (John 14:6). God insisted that I come into His kingdom in Jesus's name.

Peter says we are of a royal priesthood; we all have direct access to God, and with Him at the center of our identity, we are called to show others His goodness. "But ye are a chosen generation, a royal priesthood, an holy nation, a peculiar people; that ye should shew forth the praises of him who hath called you out of darkness into his marvellous light" (1 Peter 2:9).

So if He chooses you and you obey His calling, your identity will become being a soldier and a warrior of God. Being a warrior in the Spirit is far greater than being a natural warrior; God is entrusting us to deal with the Enemy in the spiritual realm.

When God the Father chooses us, He knows exactly what He is doing. It doesn't matter to the Father if your former identity was a member of the military or an agnostic, an atheist, a Jewish person, a Muslim, etc. God can call anybody to change their ways and follow Him. He does the choosing. John 6:44 says, "No man can come to me, except the Father which hath sent me draw him: and I will raise him up at the last day."

God can call people who seem the most unlikely. While I was in the US Army, I did not care and had no ambition. But in God's army, I care exceedingly. The Lord Jesus through Holy Ghost has a way of making a person care. It is all about Him and not about me.

The apostle Paul, originally Saul, spent his time persecuting and killing Christians. Yet God spoke to him on the road to Damascus, and he became one of the most preeminent leaders of the Christian church. He was definitely as unlikely a follower of Christ as you could get. Paul is credited for spreading the gospel and is said to have traveled over 10,000 miles on his missionary journeys.[10] He risked his life for Jesus, becoming shipwrecked, beaten, and jailed for his love for the Lord. Paul answered God's calling and became, without a doubt, one of the Lord's greatest warriors.

During my time in the military, there were several times when I felt unqualified and even unwanted. When I was in basic training/boot camp, the authorities asked for volunteers to go Airborne, and I signed up. I did the extra PT and a lot of running, but they never allowed me to join Airborne. Many years later, I spoke to a friend of mine with some background into the situation. I asked him if

I wasn't chosen for Airborne because of my lack of education. He said no. But I did tell him I had scoliosis, or abnormal curvature of the spine. He then assured me that the scoliosis was the reason. By the way, this friend was NSA (National Security Advisor) before he was Delta Force. A second friend who is a pastor in Oklahoma and was a jumpmaster in Airborne told me the same thing. A third friend in Louisiana, who was Delta Force, also confirmed the reason preventing me from entering Airborne. He said it does not take a genius to jump out of an airplane. By the way, all those friends of mine are born-again believers in the Lord Jesus Christ. What warriors we have in this wonderful nation of ours!

Father God called all types of people to Himself—educated, uneducated, scoliosis or not. Like the Scripture says in Hebrews 3:15, "While it is said, To day if ye will hear his voice, harden not your hearts, as in the provocation." Nothing disqualifies you from being a soldier of God. But as soldiers, we need to live up to our calling.

I remember one time in Vietnam when I seemed to have forgotten I was a soldier for a brief minute. We were near Dong Ha, which is near the demilitarized zone (DMZ). This place was flatland—not jungle not rice field—simply flat. We ran across a few Vietcong and were fired upon, so we then returned fire. One man at whom we were shooting kept running. Then, suddenly, he went behind this mound of dirt and disappeared. It must have been a tunnel. Everyone on my track was shooting at this guy and missing. Then, out of nowhere, a soldier from New York took my rifle out of my hands and started shooting at the guy, who still kept running. I was stunned and got my rifle back. I marveled at how that NVA soldier disappeared, but I was also humbled that I had allowed that man to take my rifle. As Christians, don't give up your identity in Christ or your weapons.

That same day, we captured five Vietcong and tied them up. Then a chopper landed in the area. And suddenly this colonel got out of the chopper and started to separate the captured Vietcong. I thought, "What does this guy have to do with this situation?" There was no need for him to drop in unannounced, telling us how to do our jobs. Some people want to stick their noses in where they do not belong. I have no understanding of that colonel's action at all—none.

When I was in the army, I liked being a soldier, but some people messed me up with their actions, like that colonel dropping in and ordering us around. As Christians, don't let others discourage you. I am more military minded now because of the Lord Jesus than I was when I was in the army and even in Vietnam. Today, I am militant for my Lord, His soldier warrior. He makes the difference by His blood, the blood of the Lamb of God slain from the foundation of the world (Revelation 13:8).

I've had times in my life when I wasn't confident in my identity and who I was. I had a friend who had off-the-charts intelligence. I asked God the Father, "Why does this guy want to hang with me?" He told me that it was because of the anointing, my military background, and my time in Vietnam. But the bottom line was that the Lord was drawing him to me. The Lord Jesus wanted my friend to have the baptism in the Holy Ghost with the biblical evidence of speaking in tongues. What a God we serve! Learn from me and don't doubt your worth.

Martin Luther is an example of someone who was confident in his identity as a child of God and committed to the works the Lord wanted of him. Martin Luther was one of the greatest Germans known because he knew Jesus the Christ. That German Roman Catholic priest knew the Lord Most High. Martin Luther was a Roman Catholic priest known as the Great Reformist. In the fifteenth century, he began to reform the way Roman Catholics worshipped God. There were a few before Martin Luther who wanted reform, but God wanted Martin Luther to succeed, and he did. He was a Roman Catholic priest who married. Praise the Lord Jesus for Brother Martin.

There are many officers whom I encountered in my three years in the Army—some good, some not so good, some trying to make a name for themselves. As God's children and warriors, we are called to do work in His name—not to make a name for ourselves. But it does, of course, happen even in the ranks of Christianity. The Lord Jesus never did that. He would conceal Himself—do miracles, signs, wonders—then He would tell the people not to say anything. But the people would go out and tell everybody.

To enable me to become more like Jesus and less like those selfish officers I mentioned earlier, God has worked in my life to ensure that I learn humility and that I do not make a name for myself while also teaching me my identity in Him. One of the ways that He is accomplishing this work in me is by giving me promises via prophetic messages and then choosing to delay those promises from coming to pass for decades. Over the past several years, I compiled a collection of prophecies into a notebook that other trained prophets have prophesied over me. Some of these prophecies were given to me around thirty years ago and have not come to fruition yet, such as prophetic words saying that I would become a preacher. I've gotten impatient at times waiting for many of these promises—especially God's promise for me to be a preacher—to happen. But all parts of God's body are crucial to its functioning, and I continue to trust in the work God has me doing right now. I also trust that the Lord will cause me to experience more of my identity in Him by bringing these promises to pass while still working to ensure that I remain humble.

★ ★ CHAPTER 11

DELIVERANCE

And he said, The L*ORD* *is my rock, and my fortress, and my deliverer.*
2 Samuel 22:2

IN THE 1980S, I HAD anger issues. I knocked holes in our walls and slammed things around. My beautiful wife, Sheila Ann, noticed I had a pattern of anger for no apparent reason. We had never heard of post-traumatic stress disorder (PTSD) caused by the effects of war. No one informed us of this. At times, I would weep for no reason.

After my anger issues and then a panic attack, Sheila and I eventually went to the Veterans Administration for help. The psychiatrist was of no assistance though, so we had to go to an outside source. He said, "Oh, you have PTSD." Consequently, I am considered by the US Government to be at 100 percent disability due to my war wounds and PTSD, and I'm compensated well for my service to my nation. However, I most regret that my kids felt the brunt of my PTSD, but I know that Father God will make them stronger and greater for it.

PTSD wasn't recognized as a mental health condition until 1980, and Vietnam vets were the first veterans to be diagnosed with the term PTSD. According to the US Department of Veteran's Affairs, approximately 30 percent of Vietnam vets experienced PTSD.[11] I'm surprised though that the statistics are only at 30 percent. We were not in constant battle in Vietnam, but we were always on the alert, hence the PTSD. This disorder is real. Anybody who has been in combat can understand this affliction. In war, there is a hypervigilance—always looking for something to take place, on the alert. And with soldiers in battle, it is a given that we will help. So with PTSD, there is a constant feeling of being unsafe.

Many people may not understand PTSD. I did not at first. My dad fought in World War II, and I now realize he suffered from PTSD as well. At that time, they called it shell shock. My dad did not understand at all the toll that war had taken on him. PTSD comes out differently in people. For my dad, his PTSD manifested itself in alcoholism and a love for bar fights. He was an alcoholic and died of cancer at fifty-four years old. He kept everything in and very rarely talked about his war experiences. I wish he could have received therapy, like I did. And I wish he would have received help from the Lord Jesus Christ. We cannot deal with our issues on our own. God wants us to lean on Him for help.

Before I became a Christian, I did not speak much about my time in Vietnam. The Lord has helped me to realize, though, that I need to talk about it and that it's OK to get emotional about it.

Today, my PTSD has been mostly straightened out, but there are still remnants. Since I accepted Jesus that September day in 1975, He started to deliver me little by little from this disorder. Emotional things take a long time for deliverance. But with the help of the Lord Jesus—the Most High God—my wife, my children, and prayer, I am conquering this disorder. I've prayed earnestly for the Holy Spirit to help me in my weakness. God is the source of all my help.

Paul the apostle wrote to the church in Ephesus saying, "Be ye angry, and sin not: let not the sun go down upon your wrath" (Ephesians 4:26). Father God will work through His saints. His ministers are a flame of fire. Self-control is a key to getting things right with the Lord. God the Father drew me into His kingdom, and I am grateful that He can help me with the effects of war.

As I mentioned earlier, self-control (temperance) is one of the fruits of the Spirit, and I've learned that I gain those fruits only by leaning on Him. I simply cannot do it on my own. I am thankful for His grace and patience with me as He delivers me from PTSD and helps me to become identified with more of the fruits, such as self-control, patience, peace, and joy, as I conquer and experience victory and deliverance from PTSD. I love to laugh and find that the joy of the Lord is my strength (Nehemiah 8:10).

Deliverance—what a powerful ministry it is. My wife and I walk in this ministry even this day. Though my wife and I are ordained ministers, the deliverance gifts He gave us, before we were ordained, remain. God's Word is sure and true. Romans 11:29 says, "For the gifts and calling of God are without repentance."

My wife and I had a deliverance ministry in the 1980s. People would come to our home with many different struggles, sins, or sicknesses, and we would intercede in war against the forces keeping these people down. Many people experienced deliverance and felt evil forces leave them, and others were delivered from addiction.

There are times when physicians, nurses, and psychologists of all kinds can provide extraordinary aid to our lives. I believe all soldiers need help after combat. Counseling can help veterans to have the mind of Christ and be strong-minded people. First Corinthians 2:16 says, "For who hath known the mind of the Lord, that he may instruct him? but we have the mind of Christ." The strongest help we can get comes from above, from the Lord Jesus, who intercedes for us to the Father.

I experienced profound encouragement recently when a pastor at our church, who was a master sergeant in the US Army, laid hands on me and told me he was praying for my mind because of the things I had experienced in Vietnam. This was a powerful word to me the Lord spoke through him and brought me encouragement that God will finish the work He has started in me.

Fellow military, God can help deliver you from PTSD. There are many ways for this deliverance. My deliverance came from above, and as I have said, it is not an overnight healing, as I would have wished. But God provides medical and psychological experts to also help deliver us. Keep in mind that when a counselor knows Jesus as Lord and Savior, the veteran and the counselor will be working off the same page. Veterans ought to work with someone who will give credit to the Most High God and not himself or herself.

I am not laying blame, but the VA psychiatrist should have seen something when I visited rather than me having to seek outside help. The Veterans Administration is a great organization that helps many veterans throughout this country, but it needs to be adjusted from time to time.

Father, I pray in the name of Jesus that you would help the VA see the need of all our veterans, past, present, and future. We need a strong military now, and always. We need a strong VA as well. I think there are good things in store for our VA and healthcare. We are beginning to see positive changes with the help of a good president as of the 2016 election. Even now, I can go to my chiropractor without having to pay for it. I am grateful when this country looks out for its veterans. God is in charge; He is sovereign. This is His earth and the fullness thereof.

I pray that all the military would call upon Jesus the Christ. I say it again—this whole nation needs Him. God the Father will answer you if you call on the name of Jesus. You do not have to do it aloud, but you must do it from your heart. And we as believers in Christ have a duty to pray for the physical and emotional well-being of our current military and the emotional wellbeing of our country's veterans.

★ ★

CONCLUSION

THE VIETNAMESE HAD BEEN FIGHTING a war for twenty-five years before we got there, and they were tenacious. They fought the Japanese, the French, and the Americans. I admire the tenacity of an enemy who will not quit, even against a superpower like the United States. Unfortunately, politics entered the Vietnam conflict, and we lost the war. President Ho Chi Minh wanted all of Vietnam to be communist, and he got it. But I do believe that it was our duty to try to stop communism. It is my belief that although we lost the war, eventually communists would have tried to take over the United States of America. Think about the attacks that happened on September 11, 2001. We went after the terrorists to put a stop to terror! John Paul Jones, a naval commander in Revolutionary War days, said, "He who will not risk, will not win." The Lord Jesus risked all.

I love my nation. Truly, God has shed His grace on America. We are oh so blessed to live in a democracy and not under communist rule, where everything goes to the government and the people are not free. In the United States of America, we are free, but we cannot do anything we want to do. Laws govern us, some good, some not so good. For instance, we can drink alcoholic beverages but not drive. This is a good law. We are a free people, and we have the right to bear arms against enemies of our nation. As citizens, we have the right to have guns in our homes. Any laws that prohibit firearms in the home is wrong. I fought for that freedom; many died for that freedom.

I am so grateful to all the men and women who took part in all the wars the United States has fought. To lay down one's life for another is a special trait that comes from above. And it's not talked about much, but there have been many Christians killed for their belief in Jesus Christ over the centuries. I believe that there will be many more as well. Remember that this is war.

I also thank all the men and women who serve the Lord Jesus and are soldiers and warriors for our God. We have a great army: the host of God the Father, the Lord Jesus and Holy Ghost. We honor the Lord Jesus because He is God.

If you are a patriot, you admire those who have given their lives for our country. Jesus gave His life for all of mankind, but Satan doesn't want you or me or anyone to believe and have faith in Christ. The Bible says that Satan is the god of this world and blinds the mind of the unbeliever. 2 Corinthians 4:4 says, "In whom the god of this world hath blinded the minds of them which believe not, lest the light of the glorious gospel of Christ, who is the image of God, should shine unto them." Satan goes to war with us to keep us unbelievers, make us doubt, or make us sin.

I believe that Holy Ghost wants you to know what is required of you and this whole country because He wants to bless us here. Second Chronicles 7:14 declares, "If my people, which are called by my name, shall humble themselves, and pray, and seek my face, and turn from their wicked ways; then will I hear from heaven, and will forgive their sin, and will heal their land." This word applies now.

Father God gave me a vision for You, beloved reader. At 0630 hours, September 19, 2019, the hand of the Lord came upon me. I saw in a vision that God the Father had a huge foot tub in His hand and was pouring out blessings upon the earth for His people. Remember, He has a remnant, and they will do exploits for their God. I saw that many miracles would begin taking place. The Father of all glory is doing this for His people, for He desires to bless His people who will be soldiers and warriors for Him. These soldiers will do exploits for the Father, because He is doing these exploits through them in this day, saith the Lord! So take no thought about how this is to come about.

There is coming a time when many disasters will come, saith the Lord! In my vision, the Lord said, "Surely, they will look to Me to change things around. But I am looking for them to change their minds to come into Me and be saved, so I can be their God and Savior. It is what I am all about; I came to save the world. But the world is still rejecting me. So I am loosing many things upon the earth, blessings that they may see and disasters so that they may come to me." The Lord says, "I want My house; I want My house full."

I believe that as God's children, we sometimes want to rebel, but Father God is long-suffering, patient. He waits long for His children to be obedient, that He may bless them. So Beloved, if you find yourself in a rebellious state, repent. Turn away from your wicked ways and come to the Lord Jesus. John 6:37 says, "All that the Father giveth me shall come to me; and him that cometh to me I will in no wise cast out." The people of this land of ours that I love need to be healed with the help of our Lord. He is our Helper. To heal, we need to hear what saith the Lord. We need more military officers who get their orders from God. If an officer did declare that he or she received orders from the Lord, that officer would probably be sent to a psychiatrist for an evaluation. But if military leaders would pray to God the Father in the name of Jesus and get their instructions from Him, this nation would be better off. This nation that I love needs to change and call upon the Lord of all glory, the Lord Jesus, the Christ, the Son of the Living God. If this nation would become subject to God's laws, then things would change for the better.

As God's called seer and prophet, I am committed to do His will. His vision came upon me, and He told me to write the vision that I shared earlier for this book. I believe that Father God desires obedience more than anything else. He is God, the Lord Jesus, and Holy Ghost. He wants obedient servants to be His disciples, His true followers.

James 1:22 exhorts, "But be doers of the word, and not hearers only, deceiving your own selves." That word applies to me and all fivefold ministers, and to everyone who calls upon the name of the Lord Jesus. We are to be obedient to His Word.

Father God is so good. He is leaving us a message to remember. Malachi 4:1 states, "For, behold, the day cometh, that shall burn as an oven; and all the proud, yea, and all that do wickedly, shall be stubble: and the day that cometh shall burn them up, saith the LORD of hosts, that it shall leave them neither root nor branch."

Listen, Beloved. We serve an awesome God who is sovereign. All the world needs to know that. He loves His body, the church. Remember, the Scriptures teach God is the same yesterday, today, and forever. Hebrews 13:8 says, "Jesus Christ the same yesterday, and to day, and for ever." The Lord Jesus is God and worthy of our love, obedience, honor, and commitment.

Beloved, pay attention to Malachi 4:2: "But unto you that fear my name shall the Sun of righteousness arise with healing in his wings; and ye shall go forth, and grow up as calves of the stall." Can you say "Amen"? This is God's Word for the ones who revere His name.

Finally, Holy Ghost wants to write to you, through me, the names of God. These are just a few, but it explains whom we serve.

NAME	MEANING	SCRIPTURE
Elohim	Strong	Genesis 1:1
Adonai	My Lord	Exodus 4:10–13
Elyon	Most High	Genesis 14:20

El Roi	The Strong One who sees	Genesis 16:13
El Shaddai	Almighty God	Genesis 17:1
El Olam	Everlasting God	Isaiah 40:28
Yahweh	Lord I Am	Exodus 3:13

Beloved reader, please receive my words with an open mind, that Holy Ghost would come upon you and that God would draw you into His kingdom. I leave you with Numbers 6:24–26: "The LORD bless thee, and keep thee: The LORD make his face shine upon thee, and be gracious unto thee: The LORD lift up his countenance upon thee, and give thee peace."

ABOUT THE AUTHOR

Don Boudreaux served in the United States Army from 1966 through 1969 and is a combat veteran, fighting in Vietnam from 1967 through 1968. He was honorably discharged after being severely wounded, and he received a Purple Heart for his service. Don came to know Jesus in 1975 and is a called prophet and seer of the Lord. He received training in prophetic ministry from a church affiliated with Christian International and was ordained and licensed as a minister after graduating from Rhema Bible Training Center in 2005. He resides in his home state of Louisiana with his wife, Sheila, of forty-four years—who is also a called prophetess and minister—and they have been lovers of Jesus Christ and filled with the Holy Spirit for as long as they have been married. Together they are dedicated to ministering and equipping others with truth and hope through prophetic ministry. Don is a proud father of six and a grandfather of ten.

NOTES

[1] National Archives, last reviewed April 30, 2019, https://www.archives.gov/research/military/vietnam-war/casualty-statistics#category.

[2] Hope Bollinger, "How Is the Belt of Truth Part of My Spiritual Armor," December 27, 2019, https://www.crosswalk.com/faith/bible-study/how-is-the-belt-of-truth-part-of-my-spiritual-armor.html.

[3] Dave Johnson, "What Is the Breastplate of Righteousness?," https://lifehopeandtruth.com/change/christian-conversion/armor-of-god/breastplate-of-righteousness/.

[4] "Shoes of Preparation," Freebiblestudyguides.org., http://www.freebiblestudyguides.org/bible-teachings/armor-of-god-shoes-of-preparation-gospel-of-peace.htm.

[5] "Shield of Faith," Bible.org. 2020, https://bible.org/seriespage/24-footwear-peace-and-shield-faith.

[6] Dave Johnson, "What Is the Helmet of Salvation?" 2020, https://lifehopeandtruth.com/change/christian-conversion/armor-of-god/helmet-of-salvation/.

[7] Hope Bollinger, "What Is 'Helmet of Salvation' in Spiritual Armor?," December 16, 2019.

[8] https://www.crosswalk.com/faith/bible-study/what-is-a-helmet-of-salvation-in-spiritual-armor.html.

[9] Debbie McDaniel, "5 (Biblical) Reasons God Might Send His Angels," March 17, 2015, https://www.crosswalk.com/faith/spiritual-life/5-biblical-reasons-why-god-might-send-his-angels.html.

[10] Ryan Nelson, "Who Was the Apostle Paul," February 28, 2019. https://overviewbible.com/apostle-paul/.

[11] US Department of Veterans Affairs, last updated September 24, 2018, https://www.ptsd.va.gov/understand/common/common_veterans.asp.

Order Information

To order additional copies of this book, please visit
www.redemption-press.com.
Also available on Amazon.com and BarnesandNoble.com
Or by calling toll free 1-844-2REDEEM.

CPSIA information can be obtained
at www.ICGtesting.com
Printed in the USA
FSHW011933300621
82776FS